Mauritius: Its Creole Language

The Ultimate Creole Phrase Book & Dictionary

Mauritius: Its Creole Language
The Ultimate Creole Phrase Book

ENGLISH-CREOLE DICTIONARY

Jacques K. Lee

Nautilus Publishing Co   London

First published in Great Britain in 1999

Published by Nautilus Publishing Co
P O Box 4100
London SW20 OXN England
Tel. 0181 947 1912   Fax 0181 947 1912
Email: npc@mauritiusukworld.co.uk
Website: www.mauritiusworld.com

Copyright © Jacques K. Lee 1999

Cover design and illustrations by Richard J Lee

Printed by Ludo Press London SW18 3DG

A catalogue record of this book is available from the British Library

ISBN 0 9511296 2 7

To

Those who are striving not to forget their Creole
and all those, overseas Mauritians as well as non-Mauritians,
who are trying to learn to speak it,
if only as correctly and fluently,
as those expatriates
who claim to have forgotten their mother tongue.

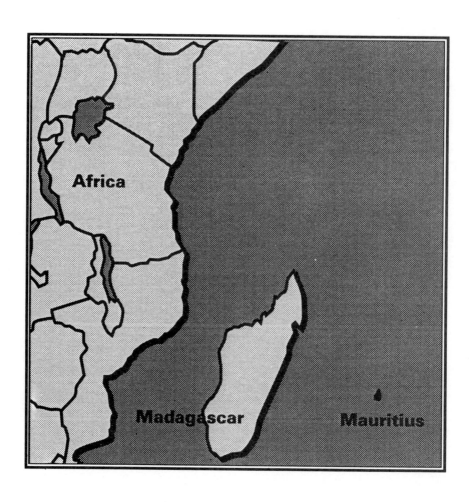

Africa

Madagascar   Mauritius

Map of Mauritius

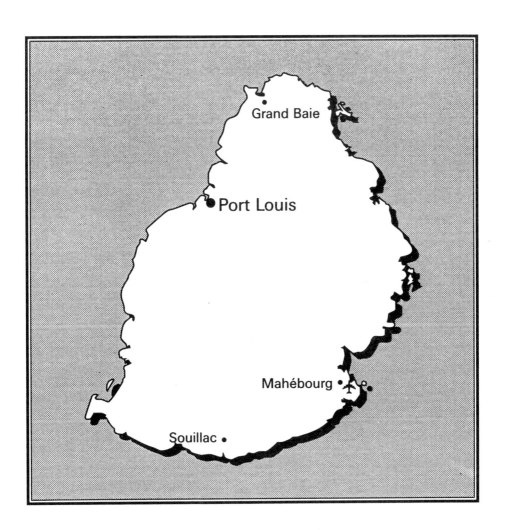

Contents

Acknowledgments   X

Introduction   1

Part One

1   THE BASICS   7
     Some essential words and examples of their uses   11
2   COMMON WORDS AND PHRASES   15
     Greetings and farewells   18
     Everyday phrases   19
     Phrases needed when in difficulties   21
3   ARRIVAL IN MAURITIUS   22
4   AT THE HOTEL   24
5   EATING AND DRINKING   26
     Glossary of restaurant and food-related terms   28
     Some Creole pertinent words and terms   30
     In the restaurant   31
     Local fruits, vegetable and spices   33
     Creole names of local ingredients and fruits   34
     Creole names of local edible fish   35
6   MOTORING AND PUBLIC TRANSPORT   36
     Relevant vocabulary   38
7   GOING SHOPPING   41
     Useful words and phrases   42
8   FAMILY, RELATIONSHIPS AND PEOPLE   45
     Creole appellations   46
9   SIGHTSEEING AND SPORTS   49
10   HEALTH   52
11   FLORA AND FAUNA   56
     Introduced species   57
     Domestic and wild animals and birds seen in Mauritius   59
12   MISCELLANEOUS   60
     Weight & measures and semi-technical words   60
     Tools; Housing terms   61
     About the house; The office   62
     Religious festivals and anniversaries   63
     Musical terms   64

Part Two

13   CRAZY CREOLE   **67**
              Crazy numbers - numerical slang   70
              Creole rhymes   71

14   CREOLE IDIOMS, INTERJECTIONS AND SLANG EXPRESSIONS   **73**

15   A TASTE OF MAURITIUS   **81**
              Mauritian gastronomy   81

16   RECENT ADDITIONS TO CREOLE   **88**

17   CHILDREN'S CREOLE   **92**

18   CREOLE CREOLE   **93**

19   ARCHAIC FRENCH   **95**

20   TRUNCATED FRENCH   **96**

21   NOT IN FRONT OF THE LADIES (OR CHILDREN)!   **97**

22   THE HISTORY OF MAURITIUS AND ITS LANGUAGES   **100**

23   DICTIONARY — ENGLISH-CREOLE   **119**

24   BIBLIOGRAPHY   **148**

Acknowledgments

I would like to extend my deepest gratitude to every one who has given me help, assistance or advice during the writing, compilatioin and preparation of this book. Without singling out any one in particular they are, in alphabetical order, Jeremy Collins, JohnCollins, Jane Dickinson, Adrienne Fell, Vivienne Henry, Tony Zurbrugg and members of my own family. I am equally indebted to them all.

Grateful acknowledgment is made to Dr Philip Baker for generously sharing his expertise on Mauritian Creole over the years and for the various references to his two books: *Kreol* and *Dictionary of Mauritian Creole*. I am also indebted to the Mauritius Tourism Promotion Authority for permission to reproduce the cover photograph and for the enthusiastic collaboration of its London Manager Sohun (Toto) Ghoorah and his assistant Emilie Leong Kow. Last but not least, the sponsorship of Air Mauritius is gratefully acknowledged.

INTRODUCTION

The main objective of this book is to acquaint visitors to Mauritius with Mauritian Creole, the most widely spoken language on an island where over a dozen different tongues are spoken daily by the various races that live in harmony in what has been described as 'a United Nations in miniature'. This French patois or pidgin French is the language used by most Mauritians, and yet it has no official written form. It is a colourful if simple system of communication that has evolved from the days of slavery and survived to become the lingua franca of modern Mauritius.

Visiting a foreign country without knowing its language at all is like going to a museum and not reading the explanatory notes about the exhibits. Knowing a little of your host country's language not only makes your visit far more interesting, as you will get more out of it in every way, but your stay will also be more enjoyable as you will get to know the people better through trying to speak to them in their own tongue. In return, you are likely to get better treatment and be made more welcome by them. This is especially so in Mauritius, where the majority of holiday makers make no effort to speak in Creole because they know the islanders can speak English and French, amongst other languages.

This book is more than just a tourist's phrase book and as such it is also aimed at the thousands of overseas Mauritians and children of Mauritians who were born outside Mauritius. Among these are included Mauritian-born adults who left the country when they were young and who may now speak little Creole or none at all. Yet another category of people who will benefit from this book are non-Mauritian spouses, whether they have some knowledge of the language, or absolutely no idea what their Mauritian other halves are saying when talking to their Mauritian friends.

Reading this book should not only provide the meanings to often-heard words or expressions uttered by Mauritians, but should also lead to a better understanding of the Mauritian mentality, culture and heritage. Suddenly this strange language should begin to make sense!

As for those overseas Mauritian children who are planning a holiday in Mauritius and who can speak a little Creole, this book will help them polish it in no time. Not only will they surprise and delight their cousins and other relatives on the island with their knowledge, but they will no longer miss out on anything because half the time they cannot understand what is being said.

In writing this book the needs of another group of people have also been taken into consideration – those who know almost nothing about Mauritius, but who need to because they are going to live and work on the island. These expatriates will need to have an understanding of the language for work and just to get along with living in the country. Armed with this book, life in Mauritius can be less frustrating and more rewarding from Day One.

Finally this volume endeavours to make learning Mauritian Creole more than a mere chore of having to learn a foreign language parrot-fashion, to be forgotten as soon as you are out of the country. It aims to show the reader what an unusual and fascinating living language this broken French is, and above all that it is easy and fun to learn.

This book traces the origins of Mauritian Creole, its history and evolution, without being too academic about it, so that even non-linguists will find it easy to grasp. The book is divided into two sections.

Part One is for those who just want to have a 'holiday knowledge' of the language so as to be able to go shopping, order food in restaurants, and have simple conversations in Creole with the locals. It will give you sufficient understanding of Mauritian Creole to make you feel more at home.

Part Two is for those who have become sufficiently interested in Mauritian Creole to want to find out more about it.

After reading the first part it is hoped that the reader will have become so interested in this language as to want to know more, and will go on to read the next part. And for those who wish to study it more seriously and speak it like a native, the Bibliography contains a list of useful books to enable them to pursue their new-found interest.

The most encouraging thing, as far as learning Mauritian Creole is concerned, is that you need not feel apprehensive about making mistakes when speaking it – you just cannnot make any! This is a language with no grammatical or other rules, no verbs to learn, and you may write it down in any way you like! So do not be surprised to find the occasional words spelt differently on another page. As the Hon George Guibert, President of the Mauritius Council of Education, said in 1891: "The Creole patois of Mauritius is nothing but French badly pronounced and free from the ordinary rules of grammar."

Readers who know French and who have tackled phrase books before will think that Creole is probably the easiest language to learn. Mauritian Creole was originally made out of the sound of the French which slaves belonging to French settlers heard their masters speak. They simply imitated it in their own way, and Creole was born. Today about 75% of its vocabulary is still made up of recognisable French words. In the process many words have been shortened, or their correct sounds changed to make them easier to pronounce. For instance, *les yeux* (eyes) is pronounced **lizié** in Creole, *quatre* (four) is **cat**, *Jacques* is **Zac**. So for English people who find it difficult to get their tongue around some French words, here is an easier-to-speak version of that language. If you have no knowledge of French at all, after reading this book you may find yourself wanting to learn it!

But again, unlike real French, Mauritian Creole has no verbs to conjugate, no grammar to learn, no syntax or orthography, and there is no such thing as perfect pronunciation! Although there is little, if any, variation in the way Creole is pronounced, you need not worry at all if at first you cannot speak 'like a native.' As a foreigner, the islanders expect you to speak their language with a strange accent. What is more, they will be **mari conten** (see below) to hear a visitor trying to speak Creole. It will please them no end, and do not be surprised if complete strangers start giving you lessons in the street just to show you how easy it is to speak. Men be warned: in no time at all Mauritians will be teaching you a few more esoteric words! These may be more than naughty words: swear words which are quite descriptive of the female anatomy of your sister or mother, and are used quite liberally. For some inexplicable reason, male Mauritians take great delight in hearing you innocently say a swear word to another Mauritian, to watch their reactions. It is for this reason that this book contains a chapter on such words so that you do not get caught out – or can answer back in similar fashion! See the chapter *Not in Front of the Ladies (or Children)!*

This book is written in English and aimed primarily at readers in the UK, the European country which sends the largest number of tourists to Mauritius after France. As most Britons learn some French at school and are therefore familiar with French pronunciation, the Creole throughout this book is Gallicized. Phonetic spelling is used only where absolutely necessary, so most Creole words in the book are based on the French language, with some English spelling and pronunciation.

Whenever appropriate (and if known!) the origin of a word is given, sometimes followed by an example of its use. As mentioned above, three-quarters of the the vocabulary is derived from French but not everything is readily recognisable since over the centuries some pronunciations have become 'Mauritianized' or 'Creolized' or have even acquired a completely different meaning. The word **mari** is an example. It still means husband, but it is also used as an adjective loosely translated as great, very good, impeccable, incredible, fantastic, big. As Creole is a living language, it is constantly 'borrowing' new words from the languages of other communities in Mauritius. More recently, the arrival of so many foreign tourists and Mauritians who now live abroad has brought about an increase in the Creole · vocabulary, for example the use of the word *ciao* for goodbye. See *Recent Additions to Creole* for a list of such words.

The chapter *Archaic French* consists of French words used at the time of Louis XV and Voltaire but which are either no longer employed in modern French or, if they are, now have a different meaning. This is the French of the first settlers who arrived in Mauritius in the 18th century. The average French person from Annecy will not recognise many of the words in this chapter, which presents a good puzzle for linguists who are looking for a challenge on a quiet afternoon.

Mauritian Creole is a fun language, and some visitors may find it a bit crazy. See for yourself in the chapters *Creole Creole* and *Crazy Creole* for some of the wilder examples. For instance, instead of crossing a road, you jump it **(saute lari)**, perhaps because the drivers are so dangerous! For some unknown reason, many words are repeated twice, eg **kikisasa?** (What's all the fuss about?). Could this be an early influence of the Malagasy language, in which many words are similarly repeated? The sub-chapter *Crazy Numbers* will give you a good laugh, while that on *Creole Idioms, Interjections and Slang Expressions* will give you a flavour of the language.

Anyone who reads the book to the end will see how this living language came into being through necessity, and how because of its simplicity it has become the preferred language of all the inhabitants despite the fact that two thirds of the population are Indian. See how certain words have been adapted and discover the national sense of humour through it. You will love Creole for its outrageous construction. In what other language can you say something like **bon terib** (good terrible), meaning terribly good, and still make sense without breaking any grammatical rules? Nor do you need new words for superlatives: there is no single Creole word for best, for instance, and if something is exceptionally good you just say **tré, tré, tré** (as many times as you feel are justified) **bon.**

Some words given are not literal translations but the nearest available. Eg poultice, for which there is no exact Creole equivalent. A brown/black paste from

Chinese medicine called **coyok** is commonly used to reduce inflammation. In the dictionary and elsewhere **coyok** is given as the Creole of poultice.

This is truly a language that can be mastered in a matter of weeks, and if you are familiar with French, even faster. Creole has been estimated to contain about 10,000 words, but new ones are being added all the time. If during a conversation you cannot think of the Creole word for something but know it in French, say it. Three out of four times you will get it right. So you see, by the end of this *Introduction* you find you already know 75 per cent of Mauritian Creole! Just one word of warning: Creole is spoken rather faster than French, or so it seems. See *Truncated French*.

Once you have mastered Mauritian Creole, you will have no problem when visiting neighbouring Creolophone islands such as the Seychelles, Réunion and Rodrigues, where a very similar tongue is spoken. You may even be understood in faraway countries such as Haiti and Martinique, whose Creole is also French-based.

If after reading this book you still prefer to stick to English during your visit to Mauritius, the islanders will be delighted to practise that language with you, at your expense!

Before you start ...

As this book is written mainly for English-speaking readers who have some knowledge of French, some Creole words resemble English or French words in their spelling. Eg **for** (strong) and **ene cou** (once). It is important to realise that their meanings are completely unrelated to the English or French words whose spellings they share, and that in Creole **for** does not mean in the place of, on account of, and **ene cou** does not mean one neck in French. Mauritian Creole is essentially a spoken language. You should concentrate on the sounds, not the spellings

PART ONE

THE BASICS

In the *Introduction* it was said that there are no rules in Mauritian Creole, but it is essential to have some guidelines in order to understand its foundation and how it works. It is also necessary to learn its basics so that you can proceed in the right direction and have some consistency. This book is written on the assumption that readers have some basic French, although this is not absolutely essential. Mauritian Creole is based on French, and as such its fundamentals are closest to that language. However, for the purpose of learning to speak Creole, it may be more useful to forget most of the rules of the French language other than its vocabulary.

Also do not assume that all French words you encounter have the same meaning as in France. Whereas the language spoken there has evolved over the centuries, in Mauritius some of the words used by the first French settlers at the beginning of the 18th century have remained static, with the same meaning as at that time in the then Isle de France. At the other extreme, some French words have assumed completely different meanings, which could only have happened through slaves misunderstanding the words in the first place.

Readers may find it easier to remember some of the basic guidelines of Mauritian Creole, understand how they are employed through the examples given, and practise speaking it as much as possible with Mauritians. For the purpose of understanding this book and therefore gaining the most from it, bear in mind that the spelling and pronunciation of Mauritian Creole is Gallicized. The alphabet is pronounced as in French except for G and J which are pronounced **ze** and **zee** but have the same sound as Z, eg *Georges* = **Zorze**, *joli* = **zoli**, *Joseph* = **Zozef**. U on its own is as in French but in certain words it is pronounced as **ee** or **i**, eg *la rue* is **lari**, *tortue* - **torti**, *lundi* - **lindi**. Ch as in *chose* is pronounced **s** – **sose**, *cheval* - **séval**, *chaud* – **so**. Most of the time E is accented é, eg *demain* – **démin**. Where accents are used, they are pronounced as in French.

Many words whose every syllable is pronounced in French are shortened or, as the Mauritians say, 'eaten', in Creole: *quatre* (qua-tre) becomes **cat**, *livre* – **liv**, *justifiable* – **zustifiab**. This truncating of words makes them easier to pronounce. In many cases the preposition *de* (of) is not employed at all, eg *boîte de vitesse* (gearbox) becomes **boite vites**, *crème de bananes* – **lacrème banane**.

Then there is the habit peculiar to Mauritian Creole of merging most nouns with the definite article, or even adjective, to form one word. Eg *la bouche* (mouth) – **labous**, *la pluie* (rain) – **lapli**, *de l'eau* (water) – **dilo**, *bonne année* (happy New Year) – **banané.**

The explanation for this may be that when slaves heard their masters say *la table* or *la pluie*, they thought only one word had been used since they had no idea that the noun was preceded by the definite article. All this goes to explain why, as a spoken language, Mauritian Creole sounds faster than French.

Numbers are pronounced as in French except one - **ene**, two – **dé** and four – **cat**. There are some other slight variations, which will be pointed out as appropriate. But pronouncing your numbers in French is perfectly acceptable and you will not be misunderstood.

As Mauritian Creole is a spoken tongue and not a written one, readers should not be surprised to find that many words have more than one pronunciation. Some almost seem to be two different words: for instance water can be **dilo** or **délo**, stand – **diboute** or **débouter**, lemonade – **limonade/lalimonade**. Where this is the case, both are given with the most-often encountered pronunciation listed first.

Even Mauritians can be confused when an attempt is made to write Mauritian Creole down. Since it is not a written language there are no rules of orthography, and how a word is spelt depends on the writer. Some people use Gallic spelling whilst others prefer phonetics, which can be difficult to read let alone understand, when international symbols are not used or not followed.

For example, theatre can be spelt either as in French, **théâtre** or phonetically, **teat**. Thus, consulting a dictionary can be a lengthy process, if you do not give up in frustration first. Take the word Creole. If you look under C in a Creole dictionary you may not find it at all: it may be listed under K for **Kreol**. Certain phonetic spellings demand considerable imagination, eg a simple word such as *voisin* (neighbour) is spelt **vwazen** in phonetic Creole. Whilst this may be preferred by serious language students, visitors to Mauritius probably want things kept simple, which is the aim of this book.

Throughout the book the spelling employed will be as near to the French as possible, for English-speaking people. Some words may even be 'improved' to make them easier to spell and read, eg some silent letters, such as x in *voix* (voice), f *clef* (key), me in *pomme* (apple), e in *la roue* (wheel) are left out. The only accents used in spelling Creole words are acute é and grave è; and even these are reduced to the minimum so that *manière* is spelt **manierre**; ç is replaced by an s, so that *ça* becomes **sa**. All apostrophes have also been banished so that a word such as *c'est* is written **cé** and *l'enveloppe* **lenvlop**. Where two words are normally used, such as *la bas* (there), it is reduced to the simpler one word **laba**. In some cases 'local' spelling will be used, neither Gallic nor phonetic but that found everywhere in Mauritius, eg **vindaye**, pronounced **vinn dail** (a Creole fish dish) and **dhal** instead of *dal*. More recently adopted foreign words, many of which are English and owe their popularity to pop songs, business and computers, are pronounced as per the language of origin, eg computer, sorry, marketing.

A diminutive prefix often encountered is **ti** (F.slang: *p'tit*) which means small, as well as affection. Eg **Ti-Zorze** – Georgie; **ti-bonomme** – little boy, **ti-drink** – a quick drink, **ene ti cou** – for a little while.

The word **ti** is also used as a per verbal marker of the past. For example:

She/he had already gone – **li ti fini allé**

They were hungry – **zot ti gagne faim**

As explained above, since Mauritian Creole is made up of many languages, some with similar sounding words, so the same words often have more than one meaning. Examples will be given. The same word can also be both adjective and pronoun, or both verb and noun. This will be pointed out only where relevant.

One thing readers do not have to worry about is plurals. They are not used at all! Adjectives such as **boucou** (plenty), **banne** (group), **ene cantité** (a great deal) are placed in front of nouns to denote singular or plural. Eg:

There is one banana on the table – **énan ene banane lor latab**

There are plenty of apples on the table – **énan boucou pom lor latab**

Where there are several meanings to a word, these will be given according to how commonly they are used. Eg **laire** – 1. hour; 2. air; 3. tune

Some verbs have two forms: with or without the sound **é** at the end. Eg:

Enjoy yourself – **Amize/amizer bien**

Do you sell milk? – **Esqui ou vende/vender dilait?**

A common way of expressing a past action is to put the word **finn** (F. *fini*) in front of the verb; and similarly **pou** to denote future action:

I have eaten – **Mo finn manzé**. This may be emphasized: **Mo finn fini manzé.**

They will go soon – **Zot pou aller biento**

Superlatives are easy, and there is no equivalent of good, better, best. Just repeat the adjective as many times as you feel is merited, or add **pli/plis** (more) before the word:

The beach is extremely beautiful – **Laplaze la bien, bien, bien zoli**

This cake is good – **Sa gato la bon**

This mango is better – **Sa mang la pli bon**

This hotel is the best – **Sa hotel la mem pli, pli bon**

In most cases negatives are expressed by adding **pa**:

I'm well – **Mo bien**

I'm not well – **Mo pa bien**

Do you like it? – **To/** (singular/familiar) **ou/** (formal) **zot** (plural) **conten li?**

You don't like it? – **To/ou/zot pa conten li?**

Pa is also used for interrogation:

Aren't you well? – **To/ou pa bien?**

Haven't you eaten? – **To/ou pa finn manzé?**

Only one word, **qui**, need be remembered for the relative pronouns which, what, who, whom:

Which is your car? – **Qui loto pou toi/ou?**

What colour are your eyes? – **Qui coulaire to/ou lizié?**

Who is that person? – **Qui sa dimoune la?**

To whom does that bag belong? – **Pou qui sa sac la?**

Similarly, adjectives this, that, these, those are **sa**. The articles a and an are **ene**, plural **banne** (F. *bande* – group):

Is this chair occupied? – **Sa seze la occupé sa?** (F. *chaise*)

That was a nice song – **Sa ti ene zoli santer** (F. *chant*)

These buses are old – **Sa banne bis la vié**

Those birds are beautiful – **Sa banne zoizo la bien zoli** (F. *oiseau*)

The words **la, sa** (this, that, these, those, it, then) and **alor** (so, then, thus) are Mauritian favourites and are often used at the end of a sentence or question, and frequently both are employed in the same sentence:

Where are those policemen? – **Cote sa banne la police la?**
It's going to rain – **Lapli pou tomber la**
So, are they coming or not? - **Alor, esqui zot pé vini ou non?**

Do, (roughly equivalent to then) pronounced doh, is an expression often put at the end of a sentence, but only in familiar conversation:
You don't say! – **Pa dire moi do!**
Keep quiet! – **Res tranquil do!**

Mem – same, even, is frequently used in Mauritian Creole in its 'self' meaning for emphasis:
I want to see the boss himself – **Mo ou lé trouve patron la li mem**
It's he himself – **Li mem sa**
There is only one – **Enan ene mem**
Same old story – **Mem vié zistoire**
As can be seen, the pronoun **li** (F. *lui*) is used a lot. It means: he, she, it, him, her.

The expression **sétadire** (F. *c'est à dire*) meaning: in other words, so, this means, is often used by Mauritians before beginning a sentence.
Sétadire, nou bizin asté encor dipain - In other words, we have to buy more bread
Sétadire, personne pa pé vini alor - So this means nobody is coming

I, my – **mo**
me – **moi**
you, your – **to, toi** (familiar form)
he, she, it – **li** (F. *lui*)
we, our, us – **nou**
you, your – **ou** (singular, formal form)
your (plural), they, their – **zot**

POSSESSIVE PRONOUNS

Singular	Plural
my, mine – **mo/pou moi**	our – **nou/pou nou**
your (familiar) – **to/pou toi**	your – **zot/pou zot**
your (formal) –**ou/pou ou**	
his, hers, its – **so/pou li**	their – **zot/pouzot**

As you learn simple sentences, banish any fear of making mistakes – which is impossible when it comes to Mauritian Creole! And do not be tempted to fall back on English with the islanders, or you will end up speaking that instead! A mixture of Creole and French, on the other hand, is quite acceptable since that is what this spoken idiom is all about.

Where the origin of the word is not obvious, where known, it will be given and, if necessary, repeated when the word comes up again in another context, to avoid constant reference to earlier chapters. Initials will usually be used for the most common. Eg C for Chinese, E - English, F - French, I - Indian, M - Muslim. Where Indian is given as the origin of a word, this includes the various dialects spoken on the island such as Marathi, Tamil, Telegu. Muslim is used instead of Indian where this is deemed more appropriate, eg **Ramadan** (M). Since 75% of Creole vocabulary is derived from French, only those words which are not plainly evident as French will be pointed out. Where the literal meaning of a Creole word is considered useful, it is given preceded by Lit.

SOME ESSENTIAL WORDS AND EXAMPLES OF THEIR USES

Where – **coté, qui coté, cote sa**
Where is the hotel? – **Cote lotel la?**
Where is it? – **Qui coté?**
Which – **léquel, qui**
Which dress is prettier? – **Léquel robe pli zoli?**
There is/are – **énan** (F. *il y en a*)
There's a lot of people – **Enan boucou dimoune** (F. *du monde* can mean one person or a group of people)
With – **ek, et, are**
Mr and Mrs Dubois are not at home – **Misié ek madame Dibois pa lacaze**
He/she is with us – **Li are nou**
Is there/do you/can you – **Esqui** (F. *est-ce que*)
Is there a doctor in this hotel? – **Esqui énan ene doctaire dan sa lotel la?**
Do you sell postcards here? – **Esqui ou vand carte postal ici?**
One – **ene**; another one – **ene lot**
Let me see another one – **Laisse mo guette ene lot**
By, at – **cote/coté**
His bungalow is by the sea – **So campemen cote lamer**
There are buses waiting at the bus stop – **Enan bis pé attan cote bistop**
Can – **capave** (F. *capable*)
I can do it – **Mo capave faire li**
I can't make it/do it/reach it – **Mo pa capave**
As if – **comadire**
As if it were - **comsidiré**
He walks as if he is hurt – **Li marcé comadire li finn bléssé**
It was as if it were daylight – **Li comsidiré lizour**
Inside – **endan** (F.*en dedans*)
He is inside the house – **Li** (F. *lui*) **endan lacaze**
How – **coman, qui manierre**
How are you? – **Coman sa va?**
How does it work? – **Qui manierre sa marcer?**
For/belonging to – **pou**
The roast chicken is for lunch – **Poul roti la pou dézéner sa**
This suitcase is for that gentleman – **Sa valise la pou sa misié la sa**
Somewhere – **quit par**
Paul has gone visiting somewhere – **Paul finn alle promener quit par**

A copula which loosely corresponds to 'to be' in English is **été** (F. *étais*):
Where are they? – **Cote zot été?**
What is it? – **Qui été sa?**

Plural – remember that nouns in the plural remain the same as in the singular as they do not have to agree. Instead markers of plurality, such as **banne, zot**, are used.
I saw some blue and red fish in the sea – **Mo finn trouve banne poisson blé ek** (F *avec*) **rouze da lamer**
The workers have arrived – **Banne travallaire finn vini** (F.*venu*)

FORMS OF ADDRESS

The polite form of address for visitors is **misié, madame** or **mamzel** when addressing or greeting strangers, though villagers do not use these titles amongst themselves. Two thirds of all Mauritians come from Asia and are used to addressing relatives by their proper title. They are therefore more formal when addressing strangers, older people, their superiors and employers. Hence if you ask someone to call you by your first name they may refuse to do so, as they would not wish to be so familiar with you so quickly. If you were to insist, they might add a title eg **misié** John, **madame** Mary, **mamzel** Elizabeth.

When talking to a stranger for the first time, or to someone more senior than you in age or rank, it is polite to use the formal **ou** (F.*vous*) for the pronoun you. The more familiar 'you', **to, toi**, are for use when speaking with friends, relatives or children.

ESSENTIAL

today – **zordi/azordi**
tomorrow – **démain/dimin**
yesterday – **hier**
the day after tomorrow – **apré démain**
the day before – **avantierre**
the other day – **lot zour la**
day – **zour**
night – **lanuitte**
daytime – **lazourné**
in the middle of the night – **au milié lanuitte**
in the afternoon -- **dan lapré midi**
in the morning - **lématin**
morning – **gramatin**
midday – **midi**
afternoon – **apré midi**

12

late afternoon – **tanto**
evening – **lésoir/asoir**
before lunchtime - **avan manzer/dézéner**
after dinner - **apré dinner**
early - **bonnaire**
late - **tar**
midnight - **minuit**

1 - **ene**	11 - **onze**	30 - **trente**
2 - **dé/de**	12 - **douze**	40 - **carante**
3 - **troi**	13 - **treize**	50 - **cinquante**
4 - **cat**	14 - **catorze**	60 - **soisante**
5 - **cinq**	15 - **quinze**	70 - **soisante dis**
6 - **sis**	16 - **sez**	80 - **catrovin**
7 - **set**	17 - **diset**	90 - **catrovin dis**
8 - **huite**	18 - **dizhuite**	100 - **cent**
9 - **nef**	19 - **diznef**	1,000 - **mille**
10 - **dis**	20 - **vingt**	1,000,000 - **million**

When saying the time, the morning, am, is **dimatin**; the afternoon, pm, is **tanto/ dan lapré midi**; and evening/night time is **disoir**, as in the examples below:

one o'clock in the afternoon – **ene naire dan lapré midi**
two o'clock in the morning – **dé zaire di matin**
three o'clock – **troi zaire**
four o'clock – **catraire**
five o'clock – **cinquaire**
six o'clock – **sizaire**
seven o'clock – **sétaire**
eight o'clock – **huitaire**
nine o'clock – **névaire**
ten o'clock – **dizaire**
eleven o'clock at night – **onzaire disoir**
midnight – **minuit**
quarter past one – **ene naire et car**
half-past two – **dé zaire edmi** (F.*et demie*)
quarter to three – **troizaire moin car**
five o'clock on the dot – **cinquaire lor coco**
minute – **minit**
second – **ségone**
hour – **naire/laire**
in one hour – **dan ene naire**
in four hours' time – **dan catraire ditan**
at least two hours - **au moin dézaire tan**
at about four o'clock - **catraire par la**

Monday – **lindi**		week - **sémaine**
Tuesday – **mardi**		fortnight - **quinzaine**
Wednesday – **mercrédi**		month - **moi**
Thursday – **zédi**		year - **lanné**
Friday – **vendrédi**		spring - **printan**
Saturday – **samdi**		summer – **lété**
Sunday – **dimance**		autumn – **lotone**
weekend - **weeken**		winter – **liverre**

January – **zanvier**	May – **mai**	September - **septam**
February – **février**	June – **zuin/zin**	October - **octob**
March – **marce**	July – **zuliette/ziliette**	November - **novam**
April – **avril**	August – **outte**	December - **désam**

5 July – **cinq zuliette/ziliette**
30 September – **trente septam**
1 December – **prémié désam**
2 October - **lé dé octob**

first - **prémié**
second - **dézième**
third - **troizième**
fourth - **catrième**
fifth - **cinquième**
The rest are the same as the numbers, with **ième** at the end.

COLOURS

red - **rouze**	gold - **lor**
blue - **blé**	grey - **gri**
green - **ver**	pink - **rose**
black - **noir**	brown - **maron**
white - **blan**	cream - **crème**
yellow - **zaune**	dark - **foncé**
orange - **zoranze**	pale - **pal**
silver - **larzen**	shiny - **briyan**

COUNTRIES

America - **Laméric**
Australia - **Lostrali**
China - **Lacine**
India - **Linde**
Russia- **Laréssi**
South Africa - **Sudafric**

14

COMMON WORDS AND PHRASES

a lot	ene cantité	clean	prop
about	environ	cold	frai
above	laho	congratulations	félicitation
abroad	lotpéy		
accent	accen/laccen	dirty	sal, malang
address	ladresse	during	pendan
adult	adilt		
advertisement	lannonce, ré-clame	early	bonnaire
		elsewhere	ayerre (F. ailleurs)
afraid	gagne perre	end	lafin, fini
after	apré	England	L/Angléterre
again	encor ene foi/cou	enough	assez
age	laze	everybody	tou dimoune
airmail	par avion	everything	tou
all	tou	everywhere	partou
also	aussi		
always	tou létan	far	loin
among	parmi	fire	difé
amount	montan	first	prémié
answer	réponse	flower	flaire
any	ninporte	free	gratis
		friend	camarade
bad	mauvai, pa bon		
beach	laplaze	gallery	galri
beautiful	zoli	gambling	zouer
because	parcequi	garden	zardin
beer	labierre	gift	cado
before	avan	girl	tifi
beginning	commencemen	girlfriend	copine, tidiset
behind	derrierre	give	donne/donner
below	enba	glue	lacol
between	ent (F. entre)	go	aller
big	gran, gro	god	bondié
blue	blé	good	bon
book	liv	goodbye	aurévoir
boy	garson	goods	marcendize
bribe	gous	government	gouvernemen
bundle	paquet	hair	cévé
		half	la moitié/démi/edmi
camera	camera, kodak, lapareil foto	handsome	zoli/zoli garson

15

happy	**conten**	more	**encor, plis**
hard	**dir**	near	**pré**
hat	**sapo**	never	**zamais**
heat	**salerre** (F.*chaleur*)	newspaper	**lagazette**
heavy	**lour**	next	**procin**
here	**ici**	nice	**zoli, bien**
history	**zistoire**	nobody/no-one	**personne**
holiday	**vacance, conzé**	noise	**tapaz,dibri**
hot	**so**		(F. *du bruit*)
house/home	**lacaze**	nothing	**nannié** (F. *n'a rien*)
how much	**combien/comier**	now	**maintnan**
hunting	**lasas**	nowhere	**aucaine par**
husband	**mari, misié**		
		on	**lor**
image	**zimaze**	on/off	**alimé/teigne**
important	**importan**	other	**lot** (F. *l'autre*)
in	**dan, en**	others	**lézot**
in front	**dévan/divan**	outside	**déhor**
inch	**pouce**		
inside	**endan**	pen	**plime**
		pencil	**crayon papier**
jewellery	**bizou**	perhaps	**quit foi, pétette**
job	**travail, job**	please	**sivouplé**
jogging	**jogging**		
		question	**kession**
kettle	**boulloire**	quick	**vite, dégazer**
key	**laclé**	quiet	**tranquil**
king	**léroi**		
kiss	*v.* **embrasser**,*n*.**ba**	rent	**location/loyer**
		right	1. *(side, straight)*
last	**dernier**		**droite**; 2. **corek**
late	**tar/en rétar**	road	**lari**
laugh	**riyé** (F.*rire*)	rubbish	1. **saleté;**
left	1. *(side)* **gos;**		2 *(useless)* **bagatel**
	2.**resté**	sand	**disab**
less	**moin**	sea	**lamer**
little	**tighin, piti**	seashell	**coqui/coquillaze**
London	**Lond**	small/tiny	**tipti/piti** (F. *p'tit*)
long	**long**	smile	**sourire**
lost	**perdi**	son	**garson**
lunch	**dézéner, lunch**	somebody	**quicaine**
		someone	**intel**
many/much	**boucou, ene**	something	**quiq soze**
	cantité	sometimes	**parfoi**
market	**bazar**	soon	**biento**

sorry	**pardon, sorry**
spectacles	**linette/ninette**
stamp	**timbe, estampe**
sugar estate	**tablismen**
	(F. *établissement*)
sugar factory	**lizine disic**
thank you	**merci**
there	**laba**
thing	**soze**
ticket	**biyé, tikette**
toilet	**toilet, drainaze**
too much/many	**tro boucou**
underneath	**enba**
until	**ziska**
want	**oulé**
water	**dilo/délo**
weekend	**weeken**
when	**quand**
where	**qui coté/ou sa**
why	**qui faire**
wife/woman	**femme/madame**

GREETINGS AND FAREWELLS

Good morning - **Bonzour**
Good evening - **Bonsoir**
Goodnight - **Bonne nuit**
Goodbye - **Aurevoir/bye/salam/ciao**
Hello - **Allo**
How are you? - **Qui manierre?/coman sa va?**
What news? - **Qui nouvel/qui news?**
How are things? - **Qui lapose?**
How's life? - **Qui lavie?**
How do you do? - **Encenté**
I'm very well, thank you - **Mo bien/corek/okay, merci**
I'm so-so - **Com si com sa**
I'm very pleased to meet you - **Mo bien conten faire ou connaissance**
What's your name? - **Qui ou nom?/qui ou appélé?**
Let me introduce you to my wife - **Mo introdire ou mo femme/madame**
This is my husband - **Mo introdire ou mo mari/misié**
Sorry we're late - **Sorry nou en rétar**
When did you arrive? - **Quand ou ti arrivé?**
See you later/soon - **Trouve ou talerre** (F. *tout à l'heure*)
When are you leaving? - **Quand ou pé quitter/aller?**
I'm ten years old - **Mo énan di zan**
That's fine then - **Allez bon alor**
Okay then - **Allez/ allez right**

EVERYDAY PHRASES

Thank you very much - **Merci boucou/bien**
That's all right/don't mention it - **Pa ditou/padquoi** (F.*pas du tout/pas de quoi*)
It doesn't matter - **Pa faire nannié** (F. *n'a rien*)
Excuse me - **Exquiz moi**
Who are you? - **Qui sanna ou été?/qui misié/madame/ mamzel ou été?**
In a minute - **Ene ti momen**
Have you got a minute - **Esqui ou/to** *(formal/familiar)* **éna ene ti momen?**
Can you help me, please? - **Esqui ou /to capave aide moi ene ticou, sivouplé?**
Wait a minute - **Attan ene ticou/ti momen**
Don't worry - **Pa tracasser**
Never mind - **Blier li** (F.*oublier*)
We just arrived today - **Nou finn fek arrivé zordi/azordi**
The flight has been delayed - **Vol la finn en rétar**
We need a taxi - **Nou bizin ene taxi**
Am I disturbing you? - **Esqui mo pé déranze ou/toi?**
We're from England - **Nou sorte Angléterre/Langléterre**
I'm English - **Mo Anglai**
I'm still a student - **Mo encore ene étidian**
I'm an accountant - **Mo ene comtab**
I'm a lawyer - **Mo ene avoca**
My wife is a civil servant - **Mo femme ene fonctionnaire**
What's the matter? - **Qui arrivé?/qui énan?**
I don't know - **Mo pa connait**
What does it mean? - **Qui sa vé dire?**
I'm very grateful to you - **Mo bien réconnaissan**
We enjoyed ourselves - **Nou finn bien amizé**
This is very nice - **Sa bien bon terib/sa mari bon**
Come in - **Entrer**
Where can they be! - **Cote zot été!**
Where can I find . . . ? - **Cote mo capave trouve . . . ?**
You're right/wrong - **Ou/to corek/ou faire érerre**
You're in the wrong - **Ou/to pénan raison**
It doesn't work - **Li pa travail**
How do you say . . . ? - **Qui manierre ou/to dire . . .?**
I understand - **Mo compren**
I don't understand - **Mo pa compren**
Speak up - **Cause pli for**
I can't do it - **Mo pa capave**
I can do it - **Mo capave faire li**
I think so - **Mo croire**
On the contrary - **Au contraire**
It's not my fault - **Pa mo faute sa**
What's this? - **Qui été sa?**

It's late - **In tar la**
What time is it? - **Qui laire la?**
Will this do? - **Esqui sa okay?**
Where is the exit? - **Cote laporte/sortie été?**
On this side - **Sa coté la**
Over there - **Laba**
Don't go there - **Pa alle laba**
Can you lend me your pen? - **Ou capave prete moi ou plime ene ticou?**
Is it finished completely? - **Esqui li finn fini net?**
Can we visit . . . ? - **Esqui nou capave visit . . . ?**
I don't have any - **Mo napénan/mo na pa énan** (F. *il n'y a pas*)
In the neighbourhood - **Dan léparaze**
Are you ready? - **Esqui ou finn paré?**
Not yet - **Pancor** (F.*pas encore*)
Get ready - **Paré ou**
Here's ten rupees for each one - **A la dis roupi pou sacaine** (F. *chacun*)
We no longer need you now, thank you - **Nou népli bizin ou maintnan, merci**
We're returning to England tomorrow - **Nou pé rétourne Langléterre démain**
Can we have a look? - **Nou capave guette ene cou?**
This one/that one - **Sanne la**
What shall we do today? - **Qui nou pou faire zordi?**
I have some letters to post - **Mo énan banne let pou poster**
I need to make a phone call - **Mo bizin tap ene cou téléphone**
I need to go to the bank - **Mo bizin alle la banque ene cou**
How long will it take? - **Combien létan sa pou pren?**
Do you know what time it is? - **Ou/to connait qui laire la?**
In my opinion - **Sélon moi**
Do you like it? - **Ou/to conten li?**
I'll do my best - **Mo pou faire mo mié** (F. *mieux*)
I'm here with my family - **Mo ici avec mo fami**
We have two children - **Nou énan dé zenfan**
We're here on holiday - **Nou ici en vacance**
I'm here on business - **Mo ici lor bizness**
We're staying two weeks - **Nou pé reste pou dé sémaine**
I'm not staying long - **Mo pa pou reste lontan**
This is my first visit to Mauritius - **Cé mo prémié visit Maurice**
I come here every year - **Mo vinn ici tou lé zan**
I like Mauritius very much - **Mo bien conten Maurice**
What's the name of your prime minister? - **Qui ou prémié minis so nom?**
The people are very friendly - **Banne dimoune la bien zenti**
What is it? - **Qui sa sa?**
We're going to the airport soon - **Nou pé alle laréopor biento**
We hope to come back one day - **Nou esperer nou pou retourner ene zour**
Do contact us when you come to England - **Zot bizin contacter nou quand zot vinn Langleterre**

PHRASES NEEDED WHEN IN DIFFICULTIES

I don't understand you - **Mo pa compren ou**
Speak slower - **Cause pli lentmen**
Do you speak English? - **Esqui ou cause Anglai?**
I don't speak Creole - **Mo pa cause Creole**
Can you write it down please - **Ou capave écrire li, sivouplé**
Is there anyone here who speaks English? - **Enan quicaine qui cause Anglai ici?**
Help! - **Au sécour!**
Stop him, thief! - **Arrète li, volaire!**
Fire! - **Difé!**
Who is it? - **Qui sa na sa?**
Come quickly - **Vini/vinn vite**
Call the police - **Appel lapolice**
Where's the British High Commission? - **Cote lambassade Anglai été?**
My handbag has disappeared - **Mo caba finn disparaite**
My wallet has been stolen - **Zot finn coquin mo portefeil**
Give back my watch! - **Ranne moi mo monte!** (F. *rendre, montre*)
I've no money on me - **Mo péna larzen lor moi**
I've paid you enough - **Mo finn paye ou assez larzen**
I've already paid you - **Mo finn fini paye ou**
Where's my passport? - **Cote mo passpor?**
What do you want? - **Qui ou oulé/qui ou bizin?**
You're mistaken - **Ou finn trompé/ou faire érerre**
Leave me alone - **Laisse moi tranquil**
Go away! - **Aller!**
Get lost ! - **Foul quand!**
You're very annoying - **Ou bien ennouyan**
You're a pest - **Ou ene enmèrederre**
He ran that way - **Linn galoupe laba** (F.*galoper*)
Where can I find a telephone? - **Cote mo capave trouve ene téléphone?**

ARRIVAL IN MAURITIUS

Most visitors now arrive in Mauritius at the airport, with a few cruises calling at Port Louis, the capital. At Plaisance airport (officially called Sir Seewoosagur Ramgoolam International Airport) there is no problem with staff such as customs officers, police officers, airline personnel and assistants in duty-free shops - they can all speak sufficient English. However, some porters and bus conductors (there is no train service on the island) may not be able to converse in English with you, and they will be the first people on whom you can try out your Mauritian Creole - if other English-speaking islanders will allow you to do so before rushing to your rescue and showing off their English!

AT THE AIRPORT

This is my luggage	**Sa banne la mo bagaze**
That's my suitcase	**Sa mo valise sa**
These are all our suitcases	**Tou sa la nou banne valise sa**
I only have one bag	**Mo énan sellemen ene sac**
I'll carry this one myself	**Mo pou saryer** (F *charrier*) **sanne la moi mem**
Careful - that's fragile!	**Attention/tention - li frazil sa!**
This one isn't mine	**Sanne la pa pou moi sa**
Don't forget that one	**Pa blier sanne la**
I've nothing to declare	**Mo pénan nannié pou déclarer**
I can't find my keys	**Mo pas pé trouve mo laclé**
I've nothing of value	**Mo pénan nannié dé valaire**
I'm catching the Air Mauritius flight to London	**Mo pé pren vol Air Mauritius pou alle Lond**
Has the British Airways flight from London arrived yet?	**Esqui vol British Airways dé Lond finn arrivé?**
The plane has landed	**Avion la finn atteri**
How late is the flight?	**Esqui vol la boucou en rétar?**
Is there a bank here?	**Esqui énan ene labanque ici?**
Where is it?	**Cote li été?**
Where is the duty-free shop?	**Cote laboutique duty-free été?**
Where is the toilet?	**Cote toilet/drainaze été?**
Who is in charge here?	**Qui sa na en sarze ici?** (F. *en charge*)
Is the restaurant open?	**Esqui restauran la ouver?**
Where can I buy magazines?	**Cote mo capave asté** (F. *acheter*) **magazine?**
I'd like to hire a car	**Mo oulé louer ene loto**
I need a taxi -	**Mo bizin ene taxi**
Where can I find a taxi/bus?	**Cote mo capave gagne ene taxi/bis?**
My friends are waiting for me outside	**Mo banne camarade pé attanne moi déhor** (F.*attendre*)

How much is the fare to ... ?	Combien/comier sa couter pour alle...?
How far is it?	Qui so distance?
How long will it take?	Combien létan sa pou pren?
Go quickly, we're in a hurry	Alle vite, nou presser
How much do I owe you?	Combien/comier mo doi ou?/sa fait comier?
Is there a bus to Port Louis?	Esqui énan ene bis pou alle Port Louis?
Take us to hotel . . .	Amene nou lotel . . .

AT THE HOTEL

Even though the big hotels in Mauritius are reputed to have staff who, between them, can speak several languages, you will still need to have recourse to this phrase book when dealing with chambermaids, gardeners, cleaners, security guards and so on. You will certainly need it if you are staying in self-catering accommodation, which is normally run by a family. You are also more likely to come into contact with locals at such places.

USEFUL WORDS AND PHRASES

accommodation	**lozemen**	meals	**répa, manzer**
air conditioning	**climatizé**	mirror	**miroir, laglace**
bathroom	**lasal dé bain**	nightdress	**robe dénui**
bathtub	**bainoir**	noise	**tapaze**
bed	**lili**	office	**bireau**
bed, double	**lili bato**	picture	**portré**
bed, single	**lili colézien**	pillow	**lorrier**
bedroom	**lasam dormi**	pillowcase	**tédorier** (F. *taie*
blanket	**moleton**		*d'oreiller*)
bulb	**globe**	power point	**prize/pleg**
chair	**sèze**	pyjamas	**pizama**
chambermaid	**fem désam**	reservation	**réservation**
clothes	**linze**	room	**lasam**
cook	**couzinier, sef**	shirt	**sémise**
curtains	**rido**	shoes	**soulier**
dining room	**lasal a manzer**	shorts	**caleson courte**
dirty	**sal, malprop**	shower	**dous**
drawer	**tiroir**	soap	**savon/savonet**
door	**laporte**	socks	**sosette**
dress	**robe**	staircase	**lescalier**
drinks	**laboisson**	swimming pool	**lapicine**
handkerchief	**moussoir**	swimming trunks	**mayo**
iron	**ferre a**	switch (light)	**také**
	répasser, caro	suit	**costime**
jacket	**palto**	tap	**robinet**
jumper	**poulovaire, trico**	toilet paper	**papier toilet**
key	**laclé**	towel	**serviette**
lift	**lacenserre**	trousers	**long caleson/**
light	**lalimierre**		**caneson**
lock	**serrir**	washbasin	**lavabo**
manager	**manager**	water	**dilo/délo**
mattress	**matla**	window	**lafénette**

Take my luggage to . . .	Amene mo bagaze . . .
Where's the swimming pool?	Cote lapicine été?
There's too much noise	Enan tro boucou tapaze
Where's the restaurant?	Cote restauran été?
I've lost my key	Mo finn perdi mo laclé
What time is breakfast/lunch/dinner?	Qui laire tidézéner/dézéner/dinner?
The water isn't hot enough	Dilo la pa assez so (F. *chaud*)
You may clean the room now	Ou capave nettoye lasam maintnan
Have you made the bed?	Esqui ou finn fini faire lili (F. *le lit*)
The bulb's burnt out	Globe la finn brilé (F. *bruler*)
Close the door/window	Ferme laporte la/lafénette la
My shoes have disappeared	Mo soulier finn disparette
Can I buy stamps here?	Capave asté timbe ici?
Have you got any English newspapers?	Ou éna lagazette Anglai?
The television isn't working	Télévision la pa marcé
Room number 15	Lasam niméro quinze
The key to room 21, please	Laclé lasam niméro vinté ein, sivouplé
I've locked myself out	Mo finn ferme moi déhor
Has any mail arrived for me?	Esqui énan let finn vini pou moi?
The toilet's blocked	Toilet la finn bloqué
Have you got another room?	Esqui ou énan ene lot lasam?
We might be late for ...	Quit foi nou pou en rétar pou ...

EATING AND DRINKING

This chapter gives a brief overview of Mauritian cuisine, followed by some useful phrases as well as a glossary of food-related terms that can be used when ordering food in a restaurant. In *Part Two* of the book, *A Taste of Mauritius* looks at what is now loosely referred to as 'Creole cuisine' by the tourist industry. It is felt that this is appropriate in this language book as this part of Mauritian culture has probably made the greatest contribution to the language of the country in the last 100 years. A great many newish Creole words come from the various ethnic culinary terms, not to mention the utensils with which the food is prepared and cooked.

The Mauritian nation is a melting pot of the descendants of people from Africa, China, France and India, amongst others. With them they brought three of the world's greatest cuisines, a culinary heritage which over the years has undergone modification and refinement for the better. Today typically Indian, Chinese or French dishes may still bear their original names, but visitors to Mauritius from those three countries may not necessarily recognise these dishes that the populations of all races eat and consider as Mauritian food. Mauritian eating habits certainly reflect the cross-fertilisation and co-existence of the various races.

Something foreign visitors to the island will soon learn is that while the islanders are the most charming and friendly people one can hope to meet this side of heaven, they do have one or two faults. For example, their gullibility, their wry sense of humour, their talent for exaggeration. So when you are tucking into a Creole dish or listening to a story - beware! Take everything with a pinch of salt.

For a start, do not be persuaded to try those tiny green chillies, even if you are told they are baby ones and very mild: they are dynamite! There is a Mauritian saying: **Tipimen manze gro pimen** (a smaller person may be stronger and more capable in every sense than one who appears bigger and stronger). Another says: The smallest dogs are the fiercest. Just remember that the smaller the chilli the hotter it is; the biggest chillies are mild and may be used as vegetable. Nor should you let yourself be talked into ordering **carri No.2** in a restaurant - unless you wish to taste monkey curry!

If you see an illuminated sign reading Majestic Hotel, wait and watch the comings and goings before entering to ask about vacancies, expecting 5-star accommodation. Such establishments may be no more than the Mauritian version of 'tea rooms', called **lotel dité** (F. *l'hotel du thé*). An 'hotel' in Mauritius can be either an hotel, a restaurant or, more likely, a **lotel dité** where **gato francé**, (European style sweet cakes), Mauritian cakes and other refreshments are sold and tea served *à la Mauricienne*. But beware, if you order tea in such a place, unless you wish to try something with a local flavour. These traditional eating places serve tea in glasses, not cups and saucers; the tea comes ready sugared, probably with three spoons of it. Mauritius is, after all, a sugar-producing country.

This tea is made by stewing locally-grown tea leaves and milk powder in water, in a huge pot kept on a gas ring, so the tea can be boiling hot. You can ask the server to cool it down for you, but get your camcorder ready as this is quite a skill. The glass is raised in one hand as high as it will go and the contents tipped into another glass held in the other hand as low as possible, and the process is repeated several times without a drop being spilled. Thereafter the tea should be of a drinkable temperature.

With the arrival of tourists, some of these **lotel dité** are converting to European-style cafés, where tea and coffee may be had just as in England. As these restaurants and cafés operate *à la Européenne*, their staff also expect to be tipped!

There is no shortage of eating places on the island, and you may be sure that food plays a central role in any celebration. Wherever people congregate there will be several food vendors, from those who carry their wares in a tin case on their heads to those with huge display cases mounted on their bicycles. Not far away, you will probably be led to them by your nose, will be vendors frying Mauritians' favourite **gajak** (snacks - see below). Also typically Mauritian are **tabagie**, (pronounced **tabazi**) some of these no more than tiny cubicles, selling a variety of cakes, refreshments, cigarettes, lottery tickets, sweets and **gato francé**. Here you will see passers-by stopping to sip a white liquid by straw from a small bottle, a **sopine** (F. *chopine*). It is called iced milk, but in fact is mostly water.

Most well-known spirits are available but are very expensive, as every bottle of whisky or gin is imported. There is a wide choice of French wine, as well as wines from South Africa and Australia. There is also a good range of beers. Whilst locally-made wine is best avoided (vines are not grown on the island!), Mauritian beer is as good as any. Refined rum, made from sugar molasses, is very popular with tourists. Ask for Green Island Rum, Old Mill Rum, or Mainstay Dry Cane Spirit. The clear rum for local consumption, however, is quite another matter, so approach it with caution!

At the risk of sounding repetitious, certain Creole words have several different meanings. **Manzer** is a good example. It is a verb (to eat), but is also used to signify meal, food, snacks etc (see below).

GLOSSARY OF RESTAURANT AND FOOD-RELATED TERMS

air-conditioned	air conditioné, climatisé	fruit	fri
		gin	gin
alcohol	lalcol	glass	ver
ashtray	cendrier	goose	lézoi
		ham	zambon
bar	bar	heart of palm	palmis
beef	bef	honey	dimiel
beer	labierre	hungry	gagne faim
bill	bil/ladition	ice	glasson
boiled	boui	ice cream	sorbet
bowl	bol	jam	confitire, lazlé
bread/roll	dipain	knife	couto
butter	diberre	lamb/mutton	mouton
cake	gato	lemonade	limonade/ lalimonade
cheese	fromaze		
chicken	poul/poulet	lobster	omar
children's snack	friandiz	margarine	margarine
chilled	frappé	meal	manzer, répa
chilli	pimen	medium (steak)	bien frire/cui
chilli sauce	mazavarou (Malagasy)	menu	méni
		milk	dilait
chocolate	socolat	mint	lamente
cider	cid	monosodium glutamate	ajinomoto
cinnamon	canel		
coconut milk	dilo coco*	mustard	moutarde
coffee	café	oil	diluile
cork	bousson	oil & vinegar dressing	vinaigrette
coriander (leaves)	cotomili (I)		
crab	crab	olive oil	diluile dolive
crayfish	langouste	omelette	omlet
cream	lacrème	oyster	zuite
cup	tas	pastry	lapate
curry	carri, masala	pepper	dipoive
duck	canar	plate	lasiette/pla
egg	dizef (F. des oeufs)	pork	porc
fish	poisson	prawn	camaron/cévrette
food	manzer	raspberry	framboise
fork	fourcette	rice	diri/douri (F. du riz)
French dressing	vinaigrette		
fresh	frai	rum	rom
fried	frir	rum, coloured	eaud vie

* It is not normally referred to as milk in Mauritius but water

salad	**salad**
salmon	**somon**
salt	**diselle**
sausage	**socis**
sauce	**lasauce**
saucer	**soucoupe**
seafood	**fridémer**
shrimp/prawn	**camaron, cévrette**
smell	**loderre**
smoked marlin	**marlin fimé**
snack	**manzaille**
soda water	**soda**
soft-boiled	**mol**
soup	**lasoup**
vegetable soup	**potaze**
Creole clear soup	
with edible leaves	**bouyon brède**
spoon	**couyerre**
squid	**moorgat**
steak	**stake**
sugar, white/brown	**disic, blan/rouze**
tablecloth	**tablier**
tea	**dité**
tip	**pouboire**
tomato	**pom damour,**
	tomate
toast	**tos**
toothpick	**gratte léden**
underdone steak	**saignan**
vegetable	**léghime**
vegetarian	**vézétarian**
venison	**laviane cerf**
vinegar	**vineg**
waiter	**garson**
waitress	**serveuse**
water	**dilo/délo;**
sparkling water	**gaseze**
still water	**non-gaseze**
well done steak	**bien cui**
whisky	**wiski**
wild boar	**cosson maron**
wine	**divin**

SOME CREOLE PERTINENT WORDS AND TERMS

arrak/larak	home-made liquor. Ingredients: cocobut water, rice and sugar
bouyon	clear soup made of edible leaves
cap cap	to eat
carail	frying pan, in particular, wok
carol	home-made rum
cass palto	a strong alcoholic drink
castrol	saucepan (F. *casserole*)
couto sinois	Chinese chopper
dité lavani	vanilla-flavoured tea
douri ration	subsidized cheap rice (poor quality)
gonaze	light snack
grog	a tot (of rum)
lacouenne	pork crackling
ladob	Creole stew (F. *la daube*)
marteg	fat used in Indian cooking
masala	spices used as basis for curry powder/ another name for curry
minn frire	Chinese-style fried noodles
mo plein	I'm full up/ can't eat anymore
pain maison	a round crusty roll which got its name from olden days when they used to be delivered to the door. *Maison* = house
pilao	Indian rice dish with chicken and spices
ros carri	flat stone on which spices are ground using a **baba**, a cylindrical-shaped stone
rougaille	a national dish with tomato as a base
satini	chutney made of tomatoes, fruit or vegetable
soonouk	snoek (salted) fish
sopine	small bottle, half size of a standard bottle. (F. *chopine*). Standard size bottle - **bouteil.**
tempo™	pressure cooker
tilambic	illicit rum
toupette	measure used to serve spirits
ourite sec	dried octopus
ourite ver	fresh octopus
vindaye	Creole fish dish
zasar	pickled vegetable/fruit (F. *achard*)

Several of these terms are expanded in Part Two - *A Taste Of Mauritius.*

IN THE RESTAURANT

Do you serve lunch here?	Esqui ou servi lunch/dézéner ici?
Can I see the menu?	Mo capave guette meni la?
We're in a hurry	Nou bien presser
We'd like something quick	Nou oulé ene quiqsoze vite
	(F. *voulez; quelque chose*)
I'd like to reserve a table for two	Mo oulé reserve ene latab pou dé
My name is Blare	Mo appel Blare
I've reserved a table for four	Mo finn réserve ene latab pou cat
We'd like to try something local/Chinese/Indian	Nou oulé goutte ene quiq soze local/Sinois/Indien
Is service included?	Esqui service compri ladan?
What would you recommend?	Qui ou pou recommander?
Your good health!	Bonne santé/chin chin!
What's your speciality?	Qui ou spécialité?
What's in this dish?	Qui énan dan sa pla la?
Does it contain peanuts?	Esqui énan pistas ladan?
Has it got seafood in it?	Enan fridémer ladan?
What have you got as seafood?	Qui ou énan com fridémer?
Can you wipe the table, please	Ou capave souille (F. *essuyer*) latab la, sivouplé.
Is that good?	Esqui li bon sa?
Do you have any vegetable soup?	Esqui ou éna potaze?
What soup have you got?	Qui lasoup énan?
Do you have a wine list?	Esqui ou éna ene carte divin?
Do you serve wine by the glass?	Esqui ou vand divin par ver?
Just half a bottle of wine	Ene ti sopine divin sellemen
Is the local wine any good?	Esqui divin local la li bon sa?
Where is this wine from?	Cote sa divin la sorti?
Can we have some mineral water, please?	Dilo minéral, sivouplé
Is that sparkling water?	Dilo gaseze sa?
Mine is still water	Dilo non-gaseze pou moi
I don't eat any meat	Mo pa manze aucaine laviane
Do you do vegetarian food?	Esqui ou faire manzé vézétarien?
I'm a vegetarian	Mo ene vézétarien
We're ready to order	Nou finn paré pou commander
What's this Carri No 2?	Qui été sa Carri No 2 la?
I'd like my egg fried on one side only	Mo oulé ene disef miroir
We just want a light meal	Nou bizin ziste tifin (literally little hunger)
I don't eat any dairy food	Mo pa manze nannié avec dilait
This roll is stale	Sa dipain la rasi (F. *rassir*)
Is this dish very hot?	Esqui sa pla la bien for sa?

31

Is there a lot of chilli in the moolooktani?	Esqui éna boucou pimen dan sa moolooktani la? (I)
Do you have Bombay duck?	Esqui ou énan bomli? (I)
A little bit more	Ene tipé encor (F. *un petit peu*)
One or two (a few)	Ene dé
Do you do fried noodles?	Esqui ou faire minn frire/chow minn?
	Minn bui is boiled noodles, served with a dish or soya sauce.
Is there a public telephone here?	Esqui énan ene telephone public ici?
Where is the toilet?	Cote toilet/drainaze été?
Bring us some bread and butter	Amene impé dipain diberre
Can we have some chilli sauce?	Ou capave donne nou impé mazavarou?
Is this chilli very hot?	Esqui sa pimen la bien for sa?
Not too much chilli	Pa tro boucou pimen
This is not cooked	Sa pa finn cui
This is too salty	Li tro salé sa
This soup is cold	Sa lasoup la frai
What's for dessert?	Qui énan pou dessert?
I'm on a diet	Mo pé faire ladiette
Black/white coffee, please	Café noir/café au lait, sivouplé
Have you any local tea/coffee?	Esqui ou énan dité/café dipéy?
We'd like to try your vanilla tea	Nou oulé goutte ou dité lavani
No sugar	San disic
One sugar only	Ene disic sellemen
The bill, please	Bil/ladition, sivouplé
What's this item for 100 rupees?	Pou qui été sa cen roupi la?
There's a mistake in the bill	Enan ene érerre dan sa bil la
Check it, please	Check li ene cou, sivouplé
How much tip shall I give?	Combien pouboire bizin donner?
Are you Mauritian?	Esqui ou Mauricien?
Keep the change	Garde léreste/garde ti lamonnaie la

LOCAL FRUITS, VEGETABLE AND SPICES

avocado	**zavoca**	passion fruit	**grénadine**
aubergine	**brinzel**	peach	**pes**
		peanut	**pistas**
banana	**banane**	peas	**tipoi**
bean, green	**zarico ver**	pine apple	**zanana**
breadfruit	**fri a pain/fouyapin**	plum	**prine**
butter bean	**gro poi**	pomegranate	**grénad**
		potato	**pom dé terre**
cabbage	**lisou**		
cardamon	**laiti/élaiti**	spinach	**épinar**
cauliflower	**lisou flaire**	spring onion	**laqué zonion**
chilli	**pimen/pima**		
Chinese cabbage	**petsail, pak tchoi**	tamarind	**tamarin**
coconut	**coco**	thyme	**ditain**
coriander	**cotomili**	tomato	**pom damour,**
corn	**maille**		**tomate**
		watercress	**crésson**
dholl	**dhal**	water melon	**mélondo**
garlic	**lail**		
grape	**raisin**		
grapefruit	**pamplémousse**		
guava	**gouyave**		

jack fruit	**zac** (eaten as a vegetable when green)
leek	**poiro**
lemon	**limon/citron**
lentils	**lenti**
lettuce	**léti**
longan	**longan**
lychee	**letsi**
mango	**mang**
onion	**zonion**
orange	**bigaratte** (local Seville orange)
parsley	**persi**
papaya/	
pawpaw	**papaille**

33

CREOLE NAMES OF LOCAL INGREDIENTS AND FRUITS

awee/violet	taro root, edible tuber
banane zinzi	a tastier and smaller banana
barbara	sea cucumber
baton mouroume	drumstick, fruit of the plant
bilimbi	bitter fruit, often eaten pickled
brède	edible leaves, various: **décine, martin, malbar, mouroume, sonze, sousou, ziromon**
cambar	edible root of several plants: **patate, manioc**
caranbol	star fruit
cari poulé	a plant whose leaves resemble bay leaves, used in curry, stew (I)
coco mamzel	a coconut reputed for its water
caire dé bef	custard apple fruit
dania	coriander seed
fri de citaire/fricitaire	a bitter fruit used for **zasar** when green; its stone is spiky
grain sec	collective name for pulses
gro lani/ti lani	caraway seeds
lalo	ladies' finger
laqué lail	garlic shoots
lasauce soy	soya sauce
lécaire sousou/ziromon	young shoots of chow chow/ pumpkin plants
mangoze	bitter melon (vegetable)
manioc	cassava, edible root
masson	jujube fruit
patate	sweet potato
patisson	yellow vegetable like a squash
patol	snake gourd
petsail	Chinese cabbage
pipengaille	sponge gourd
pima confi	pickled small green chilli
safran	turmeric
samcot	Chinese root vegetable, eaten raw or in cooking
sonze	taro leaves
sousou	chow chow
téofoo	soya bean curd/tofu
téokon	tofu of firmer consistency
tipima	small chilli (hot)
zamblon	jambolan or Java plum, dark violet edible berry
ziromon	pumpkin

CREOLE NAMES OF LOCAL EDIBLE FISH
Not all have English equivalent names

Anguy	eel (freshwater)
Bouzoi	red emperor
Cabo lerbe	(freshwater)
Camaron	any shrimp or prawn. Smaller variety better known as **cévrette** (F. *crévette*)
Capitaine	
Carang	
Carpe	carp
Cato	
Cordonier	
Corne	
Dame béri	
Dorad	sea bream
Empereur	
Gouramier	
Gueule pavée	a great Mauritian favourite
Langouste	crayfish
Macro	
Marlin	marlin
Moorgat	squid
Mulet	mullet
Omar	lobster
Rouget	red mullet
Sacréchien	
Ton/bonite	tuna
Tilapia	(freshwater)
Ourite	octopus
Vieille	
Vacoa	steaker

MOTORING AND PUBLIC TRANSPORT

You will soon realise that Mauritian drivers enjoy overtaking - dangerously! They also seem to have a compulsive habit of testing their brakes. Where British drivers would slow down as they approach a corner or a red light, in Mauritius the vehicle is brought to a halt by braking furiously only at the last minute. Nor do they always indicate when they are pulling out or pulling in. So beware of parked vehicles with someone in the driving seat.

If you are a passenger in a car and can remember some Creole swear words from reading the chapter *Not in Front of the Ladies (or Children)!* You may hear the driver using a choice sample of them whenever the traffic light is red. But if *you* happen to be driving at night, be warned: some traffic lights are turned off to save electricity and wear and tear, and some drivers become temporarily colour-blind when approaching those that are not switched off, they drive through them irrespective of the colour being displayed *and* swear at the **robo** (traffic lights). Apart from that the Mauritian motorists are very skilful drivers - they have to be to survive!

A strange ritual to be seen all day long on the roads is people congregating at pedestrian crossings, **crosseer** (cross here) to cross the road. Since they can cross anywhere, why they collect at these points is a mystery since they do not expect drivers to stop to allow them to cross. Try it when you are driving. Stop at a zebra crossing and see if anybody waiting will dare to cross.

The fact that one Mauritian in five has a telephone, the largest number per head of population in Africa, is a sign of economic progress but the bad news is that six out of 100 also have a mobile phone which they like to use whilst driving! For an accident-free sightseeing drive round the island, when in Mauritius do as the Mauritians do - in one respect only. When rounding a bend, keep well in to your side of the road and *sound your horn*. Otherwise oncoming drivers may assume that there is no vehicle around the corner, so they can stay in the middle of the road and carry on chatting or arguing on their mobile phones. Pictures of head-on collisions regularly appear in the press. And do remember that it is compulsory to wear seatbelts in private cars and helmets when riding motorcycles.

There *are* some advantages if you are considering hiring a car in Mauritius. First, your British driving licence is valid for six months, driving is on the left and road signs are in English. There is only one snag with the latter: there are not many of them. Unless you don't mind seeing more sights than you planned, it is probably wiser to ask the locals for directions. Most know their island quite well.

There is really only one main dual-carriageway, from the outskirts of Curepipe, in the high central part of the island, to Port Louis and beyond to the north. Going south from Curepipe to the airport, there is a new fast road (**sémin nef**) which is mostly single carriageway. The dual carriageway is known as a motorway but many drivers treat it as a Grand Prix racing track and imagine themselves to be Jacques Villeneuve or Michael Schumacher. Petrol stations (**filling**) still have pump attendants. The price is state-controlled so it is the same everywhere, but unleaded petrol is not on general sale yet.

Public transport is good, frequent and cheap by European standards. There is no railway, and no shortage of taxis. Bus services are widespread, though if you wish to visit some out-of-the-way places it would be advisable to hire a car. It is noticeable that the public buses are usually older than their drivers, who also engage in the over-taking mania so as to reach the next bus stop before a rival bus. Your hotel can advise you as to whether it is cheaper to hire a car for a day or share the cost of a taxi with other guests. The taxi drivers know the island well, make good guides and can usually converse well enough in several languages for driver and passengers to understand each other. Readers of this guide, of course, will have no problem speaking in Creole!

This description of motoring in Mauritius should perhaps be taken with a pinch of salt, but it gives you an idea of the situation. If you still intend to experience this thrill, one final word of warning. If you love dogs, this is the place for you as there are strays all over the island. The trouble is that one of their favourite places for dozing is in the middle of the road, and they resent vehicles hooting to make them get out of the way. You either have to run them over or grit your teeth and wait for them to move away lethargically. Sometimes, especially at night when street lighting is either poor or non-existent, it is not only dogs you have to watch out for. Where there are pavements, they are so uneven and dangerous in the dark - not to mention the hazard of sleeping dogs (**licien**) - that the islanders also prefer to walk on the road.

accelerator	**accélérataire**	lorry	**camion**
axle	**laks**	lubricate, to	**grésser**
battery	**batri**	map	**map**
bicycle	**bicyclette**	mirror	**miroir, laglace**
bonnet	**capote**	motorcycle	**motocyclette**
boot	**box**	motor oil	**diluile moterre**
box spanner	**caiman**	motor repairers	**garaze**
brake	**frein**		**mécanicien**
bus	**bis**	mudguard	**gardbou**
bus stop	**bistop**	pedal	**pédal**
car	**loto**	pedestrian	**piéton**
car door	**laporte loto**	pedesdrian	**crosseer, passaze**
car mechanic	**mécanicien**	crossing	**clouté**
carburetter	**carbirataire**	petrol	**lessence**
choke	**startaire, chok**	petrol station	**filling**
clutch	**débréyaz**	petrol tank	**tank lessence**
coach	**bis**	police	**lapolice, garde**
dip stick	**lazoz**	pump	**lapomp**
dipped	**dim**	puncture	**fit** (F. *fuite*)
headlight		radio	**radio**
drive, to	**condire**	radiator	**radiataire**
driver	**soferre**	reverse	**quilé,** (F. *reculer*)
	(F. *chauffeur*)		**mette arrierre**
driving licence	**permi, licence**	registration	
engine	**moterre**	number	**niméro loto**
exhaust pipe	**lésapmen**	seat belt	**cintire**
fare	**pri**	spare wheel	**stepné**
fine	**lamane**		(E. *stepney*)
	(F. *amende*)	spark plug	**labouzi** (F. *bougie*)
free wheeling	**poin mor**	speed	**vites**
gear box	**boite vites**	speed limit	**limit dé vites**
gear lever	**lébra vites**	steering wheel	**volan**
grill	**gril**	taxi	**taxi***
handbrake	**frein a bra**	ticket	**tikette, biyé**
headlight .	**far**	traffic jam	**bousson,**
horn/hoot	**tromp/tromper**		**lemboutéyaz**
hubcap	**sopinet**	traffic lights	**robo**
ignition key	**laclé contac**	turn a corner, to	**cass contour**
indicator	**lindicataire**	tyre	**larou**
jack	**vérin**	wheel	**larou**
lock, to	**mette laclé**	windscreen	**parbrize**

I have a British driving licence	Mo énan ene permi Anglé
Can I drive in this country?	Esqui mo capave condire dan sa péy la?
Does the insurance cover me and my wife to drive?	Esqui lashirance la couver moi ek mo femme pou condire?
How much is the insurance?	Combien lashirance la?
Where can I hire a car?	Cote mo capave louer ene loto?
Is this firm reliable?	Sa compagnie la enreg sa?
How much is it per day/week?	Combien sa couter par zour/sémaine?
Can I return the car at the airport?	Esqui mo capave retourne loto la laréopor/airport?
What cars have you got?	Qui loto ou énan?
Don't you have another, better car?	Ou pénan ene lot loto pli bon?
Have you got an automatic car?	Ou énan ene loto automatic?
Has this car been serviced?	Esqui sa loto la finn fini chequé partou sa?
There's some damage here	Enan ene ti domaze ici
Can you drive?	Ou capave condire?
He drives like a maniac	Li condire comme ene fou
What's the speed limit?	Qui limit vites?
What's causing the delay?	Qui pé retarde nou la?
Has there been an accident?	Esqui finn énan ene accident?
Where can I park my car?	Cote mo capave park mo loto?
Do I have to pay to park here?	Bizin payer pou park ici?
Do you know the way to ...?	Qui simin pou alle ...?
I'd like some petrol/oil	Mo bizin impé lessence/diluile
Fill it up	Rempli li/plein li
The tyres are flat	Banne larou la platte
Check my tyres, please	Check mo larou, sivouplé
Do you do car wash here?	Ou lave loto ici?
Where's the owner?	Cote propriétaire la?
Mechanical breakdown	Tombe en panne/gagne panne
The car isn't running well	Loto la pé caroter
Do you repair cars?	Esqui ou répar loto?
I've got a puncture	Mo finn gagne ene fit
I've had an accident	Mo finn faire ene acciden
Nobody is injured	Personne pas finn blessé
What's wrong with it?	Qui so probleme?
The tyres are bald	Banne larou la finn izé
Where can I get a taxi?*	Cote mo capave gagne ene taxi?
How long is the journey?	Qui distance sa été?
How long will it take?	Combien létan sa pou pren?

*A **taxi train**, *seen near bus stops and shops, is one which operates as a bus, picking up three or four passengers who each pays their own fare. Illegal.*

How much is it?	**Combien sa couter?**
How much do I owe you?	**Combien mo doi ou?**
Don't drive so fast	**Pa condire si/aussi vite**
Can you slow down a bit?	**Ou capave alle impé pli**
	lentmen/doucemen?
We're not in a hurry	**Nou pa pressé**
Drive faster, we're late	**Alle pli vite, nou en rétar**
We must be at the airport	**Nou bizin arrive airport huitaire**
by eight o'clock	
Wait for us here	**Attane nou ici**
Come and pick us up in one hour	**Vine pren nou dan énaird tan**
We'll be back soon	**Nou pou retourner/révini ene ti momen**
Where's the bus station?	**Cote lagar bis été?**
Does this bus go to Rose Hill?	**Esqui sa bis la alle Rozil?**
What's the fare to Quatre Bornes	**Combien pou alle Cat Born?**
Can you let us know when	**Ou capave faire nou connait**
we get there?	**quand nou arrive laba?**
Where's the conductor?	**Cote controllaire la?**
You haven't given me my change	**Ou pa finn rende moi mo cas**

GOING SHOPPING

Souvenir shops are opening up everywhere but only a handful of towns are worth visiting solely for shopping. They are Port Louis (often referred to when away from it as **envil - mo pé alle envil pou faire shopping),** Curepipe (pronounced **Kirpip**), Rose Hill (**Rozil**) and Quatre Bornes (**Cat Born**). Local handicrafts may be found in the villages, outside the houses of the people who make them. One development which seems to be getting out of control is the spread of street markets and street hawkers (**marsan ambulan**) who are to be found wherever there are tourists.

The bigger shops accept most major credit cards but you will need to carry sufficient local money if you plan to buy things away from the tourist centres. The Mauritian currency is the rupee (**roupi)** which is divided into 100 cents. Money is **cas,** which also means loose change, and a two-cent coin. Some tourist shops will accept payment in sterling, French francs or American dollars, or will even accept your bottle of duty-free whisky as barter. Haggling is *de rigueur* - just halve the asking price and then negotiate. Do count your change!

The most common shops are **laboutique sinois**, Chinese corner shops, although they are no longer all owned by Chinese, certainly not in the villages. These 'general stores' sell just about everything. There are no specialist shops such as stationers and off licences but you will soon learn who sells what, or you can ask anybody. The smaller shops are known as **laboutique** and the bigger ones as **magasin**. Some have **demi gros** after their names, which implies that they sell goods at half the wholesale price - but just remember the Mauritians' gift for exaggeration!

USEFUL WORDS AND PHRASES

agency	**lazence**	local	**local, dipéy**
amount	**montan**		
antique	**antic**	manager	**manager, sef**
		money	**cas/larzen**
ball pen	**biro**		
blouse	**blouze**	nail polish	**verni**
		new	**nef, nouvo**
bookshop	**librairi**		
bracelet	**bracelet**	order, to	**pass commann**
brass	**cuive**	ordinary	**ordinaire**
button	**bouton**	origin	**lorizine**
chain	**lasenne**	painting	**peintire**
cheque	**check**	paper	**papier**
coat	**palto désou**	pen	**plime**
colour	**coulaire**	please	**sivouplé**
comb	**peigne**	postcard	**carte postal**
cotton	**coton**	pound (weight)	**liv** (really 500 grams, but price signs use lb.)
diamond	**diaman**		
dress	**robe**	purse	**porte monnaie**
earrings	**zano**	rhum	**rom**
enough	**assez**		
		shirt	**sémise/simiz**
game	**zouer**	shoes	**soulier**
gold	**lor**	shop/store	**laboutique/ magasin**
goods	**marcendiz**		
		shop assistant	**comi**
haggle	**marcender**	silk	**lasoie**
	(F. *marchander*)	silver	**larzan**
handkerchief	**moussoir**	size	**grossaire, dimension**
hat	**sapo**		
		skirt	**zip**
invoice	**factire**	socks	**soset**
item	**lartic**		
		tie	**cravat**
jewellery	**bizou**	toy	**zouzou**
jug	**po**	trousers	**long caleson/ caneson**
large/small	**gran/piti**		
leather	**cuir, lapo**	wallet	**portfeil**
list	**lalis**	wool	**lalaine**

Where can I buy...?	Cote mo capave asté...?
I'm looking for some gifts	Mo pé rode ene dé cado
Do you sell...?	Esqui ou vand...?
Do you take credit cards?	Esqui ou pren credit card?
It's too expensive	Li tro cerre
You're asking too much	Ou pé dimane tro boucou
That's cheap	Sa bon marcé
Don't want any - go away!	Pa oulé - aller!
It's too short	Li tro courte
It's too big/long	Li tro gran/long
What colours do you have?	Qui coulaire ou énan?
Give me two	Donne moi dé
I'll take one pound	Mo pren ene liv
Are the fruit sweet?	Esqui banne fri la dou?
Where are these oranges from?	Cote sa banne zoranze la sorti?
Can I taste one?	Mo capave goute ene?
It's not ripe yet	Li pancor mire
Is this made locally?	Esqui li dipéy sa?
Have you anything better?	Ou pénan nannié pli bon?
Have you anything smaller?	Ou pénan nannié pli piti?
I prefer a darker colour	Mo préferre ene coulaire pli foncé
Can you order one for me?	Ou capave commanne ene pou moi?
Where do I pay?	Cote mo payer?
Can I pay by cheque?	Mo capave paye par check?
I'll return later	Mo pou rétourner pli tar
My wife doesn't like it	Mo femme pa conten li
It doesn't suit me	Li pa alle are moi/li pa dan mo gou
Can you change this?	Ou capave sanze sa?
May I try it/them?	Mo capave seye li/zot?
Here's my address	Ala mo ladresse
We're staying at hotel...	Nou pé reste lotel...
Can you repair this?	Ou capave répar sa?
Is it expensive to do so?	Li pou coute boucou sa?
When do you close?	Qui laire ou fermer?
Are you open on Saturday?	Esqui ou ouver samdi?
I'm looking for a wedding gift	Mo pé rode ene cado mariaze
We're looking for T-shirts	Nou pé rode T-shirt
It's cheaper in the market	Li pli bon marcé dan bazar
You've got nothing that interests me	Ou pénan nannié qui interes moi
You're wasting your time	Ou pé perdi ou létan
Do you take English money?	Esqui ou pren larzen Anglé?
Can I try this on?	Mo capave seye sa?
Reduce the price and I'll take it	Baisse ou pri et mo pren li
Is that all you've got?	Sa mem tou ou énan?
I don't fancy anything	Mo pa conten nanniél

How much is it?	Combien sa?
Where can we buy local bags?	Cote énan vand tente?
Where is the nearest post office?	Cote lapos pli pré été?
I need some stamps	Mo bizin impé timbe
How much is it to send a post card to England?	Combien sa couter pou envoye ene carte postal Langléterre?
Is there a bank nearby?	Esqui énan ene labanque pré par la?
Do you have...?	Esqui ou énan...?
Do you have a map of Mauritius?	Esqui ou énan ene map Maurice?
Is it free?	Li gratis sa?
Do you sell writing paper here?	Ou vand papier a let ici?
What size is this dress?	Qui so dimension sa robe la?
Can I collect it later?	Mo capave collecter li pli tar?
It doesn't work	Li pa marcé
I'd like ...	Mo oulé...
I'd like a refund, please	Mo oulé ene remboursmen, sivouplé
I'm looking for beach shoes	Mo pé rode soulier laplaze
Have you got cheap raincoats?	Ou énan pardési bon marcé?
Are these all the sunglasses you've got?	Sa mem tou linette soleil ou énan?
Do you have any sega cassettes/CDs?	Ou énan casette/CD lor séga?
I'm just looking	Mo pé zis guetter
It's dearer in another shop	Li pli cerre dan ene lot laboutique
Can you have it delivered to my hotel?	Ou capave delivrer sa mo lotel?

FAMILY, RELATIONSHIPS AND PEOPLE

VOCABULARY

mother	**mama, mamy, maman, ma, ama**
father	**papa, pappy, pa, dadi**
grandmother	**granmère, gramère, granmama**
grandfather	**granpère, granpapa**
godmother	**marraine**
godfather	**parrain**
mother-in-law	**belmère**
father-in-law	**bopère**
brother/sister	**frère/saire**
brother/sister -in-law	**bo frère/bel saire**
older brother/ sister	**gran frère/saire**
younger brother/ sister	**ti frère/saire**
husband	**mari, misié, bonomme**
wife	**femme, madame, bonnefemme**
son/daughter	**garson/tifi**
aunt	**tante, matante, tantine, (matante** and **tantine** are also a form of address for an older woman)
uncle	**onc, tonton, ton. (ton** is also a title used to address a male older than oneself)
cousin	**cousin/ cousine** m/f.
relatives	**fami**
sweetheart	**gaté, (zenfan gaté** - a spoiled child)
bachelor	**celibataire, vié garson**
spinster	**vieille fi**
miss	**mamzel**. From middle age = **madame**
maiden name	**nom mamzel**
married name	**nom marié**
man	**zom, misié**
woman	**femme, madame**

CREOLE APPELLATIONS

aca	roadside vendor, usually cooking/frying in situ
alibaba	a crook, swindler
anguy	a slippery character, untrustworthy person
baba	1. baby; 2. a young sexually attractive woman
batiara	a useless person (I)
bado	a Seventh Day Adventist (After Paul Badaut, who introduced the religion to Mauritius)
barbelis	a body builder (E. Bar-bell)
béberre	a boyfriend, lover
bef	a stupid, useless, lazy person
bézerre	a despicable, unscrupulous person
bobok	1. a hen-pecked husband; 2. a weak-minded person; 3. an informer
bonne femme	1. a familiar term for a middle-aged woman; 2. one's wife or mother
bon homme/ bonomme	1. a familiar term for a middle-aged man; 2. one's husband or father
boug	a bloke, chap
bougress	1. a woman; 2. woman friend; 3. wife
bourzoi	one's employer, boss, superior
cafade	a woman of very dark complexion
catar	a person bad at passing exams, winning games; not necessarily just people, eg a horse that does not win any races
catoi	a Creole person (I)
coco/loco	a Chinese person (pejorative)
comi	a shopkeeper/shop assistant
cousin/cousine	also a term used to address a person of similar age, whose name is not known
couyonaire	untrustworthy person
crab	a miserly person
dézorderre	1. a troublemaker; 2. a boisterous child
divers	a prostitute
fouka	a mad man/woman
fourné	a nosey parker
foutaire désorde	a troublemaker
foutan	an arrogant person

gaga	a stammerer, dumb
gana	imbecile (I)
ganga	simpleton (I)
gosar	a left-handed person (F. *gaucher*)
gran blan	a wealthy Franco-Mauritian
gran madame/	term used by servants to address the head of
misié	a household. **Gran misié** also means a boss, an employer, a rich planter
iloi	islanders 'deported' from Diego Garcia to Mauritius
imam	Muslim priest
laré	a miser
longail	a tall person
longanis	a person practising witchcraft
laskar/lascarine	a Muslim man/woman (pejorative) (I)
macao/sina macaya	a Chinese (usually not born in Mauritius, pejorative)
macro	1. a pimp; 2. a person one dislikes
maraz	Indian priest, of Brahmin caste, his wife is known as a marazine (I)
maron	1. a fugitive; 2. **maron lécol** - to play truant
marsan	a seller, vendor (F. *marchand*)
marsan ambulan	a hawker, itinerant vendor
marsan dilait/ pistas	milkman/peanut vendor
marsan lapo	a pimp (F. *la peau*)
matlo	1. a sailor; 2. a mate, egalitarian term of address among males
mazanbic	a pejorative term for a Mauritian of African descent, a **Creole mazanbic** (Mozambique)
mazouzou	Creole girl, pretty woman
milat/milatress	a mullato man/woman, half caste
minante	an annoying person
miqué	a comic, buffoon (F. *mimiquer*)
mize	a partner (in a game)
monoir	my man, egalitarian term of address
mon père	a priest (Christian)
nasara	pejorative term for a Christian (Arabic)
nanar	a cunning person who always manages to get out of trouble. (From Bernard, a local criminal who became famous for escaping from a police trap)
nenenne	domestic servant, originally a children's nanny (F. *nounou*)

pandit	Hindu priest
papa coq	brothel keeper
pilon	1. male homosexual; 2. mortar
pinerre	one who likes punishing others (F. *punir*)
pion	messenger boy in office (Portuguese)
pitain	prostitute (F. *putain*)
pointerre/ printerre	steady girlfriend, suitor
pousari	1. exorcist; 2. Tamil priest
rajput	considered a low cast Indian in Mauritius
tayerre	a tailor (F. *tailleur)*
ti lespri	narrow-minded person
toké	a crazy person
zako	1. monkey; 2. mischievous child

SIGHTSEEING AND SPORTS

PERTINENT VOCABULARY

Climatic conditions

cloudy	niazé	river	larivierre
cold/chilly	frai	rock	ros
cyclonic	létan cyclone	sand	disab
heat	salerre	sea	lamer
hot/warm	so	sky	léciel
humid	himid	south	lésud
lightning	zéclair	spring	printan
misty	brimé	stone	ros
rain	lapli	sugarcane field	caro canne
rainbow	lacanciel	tide	lamaré
showers	lapli	town	lavil
storm	tempette	village	vilaze
sun	soleil	waves	vag
thunder	loraze	west	louest
weather	létan	winter	liverre
windy	diven	wood	boi

Seasons & Geography

autumn	lotone
bay	labai
beach	laplaze
boulders	ros (F. *roche*)
bridge	pon
coast	lacote
current (*sea*)	couran
east	lest
forest	laforet
hill	montagne/ ti montagne
lake	lac
mountain	montagne
north	lénor
pebble	cayou
reef	récif

Things to see

bridge	**pon**
building	**batimen**
castle	**sato**
church	**leglize**
country	**lacampagne**
crater	**craterre/trou**
cycle racing	**lécourse bicy-clette**
gallery	**galri**
garden	**zardin**
historic site	**sit historic**
market	**bazar**
monument	**monimen**
museum	**mizé**
pagoda	**pagod**
sugar factory	**lizine disic**
temple	**temp**
waterfall	**cascad**

Sports

bet	**pariaze**
deer hunting	**lasas cerf**
fishing	**lapes**
fishing rod	**lagolette**
flippers	**lapatte canar**
horse	**séval** (F. *cheval*)
horse racing	**lécourse séval**
hunting	**lasas**
jockey	**zoké**
player	**zouair**
racket	**raquette**
reggata	**régat**
scuba diving	**laplonze soumarine**
swimming	**nazer/natation**
swimming pool	**lapicine**
table tennis	**pinpong**

Most names of sports do not have Creole equivalents and the English or French terms are used. Eg golf, tennis, football.

What excursions are there today?	Qui exquirsion énan zordi?
How long will it take?	Combien létem sa pou pren?
Will there be commentary in English?	Esqui pou énan commentaire en Anglé?
We'll need a guide	Nou pou bizin ene guide
Do I buy the tickets here?	Esqui mo asté tikette ici?
Is it necessary to make a reservation?	Esqui li necéssaire pou faire réservation?
Can I go on foot?	Esqui capave marcer aller laba?
Which way is it?	Qui coté li été?
I'm lost	Mo finn perdi
Is it open on Sunday?	Esqui li ouver dimance?
Do we have to pay to go in?	Esqui bizin payer pou rentrer?
I want to take some photos	Mo oulé pren eindé foto
Will we need a map?	Esqui nou pou bizin ene map?
Which is the way to the beach?	Qui sémin pou alle laplaze?
Is it safe to swim here?	Esqui li pa danzéré pou nazer ici?
How deep is it?	Qui so profonderre?
Is this drinking water?	Esqui sa dilo la potab sa?
How much farther is it?	Esqui li encor bien loin?
Are there any dogs?	Esqui énan licien?
The weather is gorgeous!	Létan la zoli!
It's very hot today	Faire so terib zordi
It's not very cold today	Pa aussi frai zordi
It's going to rain	Lapli pou tomber la
The sun is too hot	Soleil la tro for
The rain won't last	Lapli la pa pou direr
The weather is bad this morning	Létan la mauvai cématin
We'd like to see some village life	Nou oulé quette impé lavie dan vilaz
What's worth visiting?	Qui vo lapeine visiter?
Let's go by taxi	A nou alle par taxi
It's very windy	Enan boucou diven
Is a cyclone expected?	Esqui pou énan cyclone?
Are we in the cyclonic season?	Esqui lasaison cyclone la?
Look at that double rainbow!	Guette sa doub lacanciel la!
There are a lot of big boulders in the sugarcane fields	Enan boucou gro ros dan banne caro canne
What's the name of that mountain?	Qui sa montagne la so nom?
This beach has too many pebbles	Sa laplaze la énan tro boucou cayou
Which town is older?	Lequel lavil pli vié?
Let's visit that one	A nou visit sanne la
There's not much to do here	Pénan gran soze pou faire ici

HEALTH

THE BODY

arm	**lébra**
bladder	**vési**
body	**lécor**
brain	**lacervel**
breast	**tété, sein**
cheek	**lazou**
chest	**poitrine, ches**
ear	**zoreil**
eye	**lizié**
face	**figire**
finger	**lédoi**
foot	**lipied**
hand	**lamé**
head	**latète**
heart	**lécaire**
intestine	**lintestin**
kidney	**lérin**
knee	**zénou**
leg	**lazam**
lips	**lalève**
liver	**léfoi**
lung	**poumon**
mouth	**labous**
muscle	**musc**
nail	**zong**
neck	**licou**
nose	**néné**
shoulder	**zépol**
skeleton	**eskélet**
skin	**lapo**
stomach	**lestoma**
throat	**lagorze**
thumb	**pouce**
toe	**lédoi lipied**
tongue	**lalang**
tooth	**léden**
vein	**laveine**

PERTINENT VOCABULARY

abcess	**absé**
allergy	**alairzi**
antiseptic	**antiseptic**
appendix	**lapendicit**
aspirin	**aspirinne**
asthma	**las**
back	**lédo, lérin**
bandage	**bandaze**
bitten	**mordé, piqué**
blister	**clos**
blood	**disan**
boil	**bouton, coulou**
broken	**cassé**
bronchitis	**bronsit**
bruised	**vinn blé**
burn	**brulire**
cancer	**cancerre**
chicken pox	**varicel**
cold	**lérim**
colic	**colic**
constipation	**constipation**
contraceptive pill	**pil contracep-** **tive**
cough	**tousser**
cough mixture	**siro tousser**
cramps	**lacrampe**
cut	**coupé**
death	**lamor**
dentist	**dentis**
diabetes	**diabète**
diabetic	**diabétic**
diarrhoea	**diaré**
diet	**ladiette**
disinfectant	**dézinfectan**
dizziness	**vertize**
doctor	**doctaire, medcin**
drug	**drog**

ear wax	caca zoreil	paralysed	paralizé
eczema	leczéma	pill	pilil
emergency	ene ca irzen	poison	poizon
epilepsy	épilepsi	poultice	coyok
eye discharge	caca lizié	pregnant	enceint
eye drop	goutte pou lizié	prescription	lordonance
faeces	caca	radiography	radiografi
fainted	perdi connai-ssance	remedy	rémede
		respiration	respiration
fever	lafième	rheumatism	rématis
flu	lagrip	saliva	lacrass
haemorrhoids	hémoroid	sleep	dormi
hayfever	lafième dé foin	smell, to	senti
headache	latète faire mal	sunglasses	linette soleil
health	lasanté	suntan lotion	lotion soleil
high blood pressure	tension	swelling	enflé/gonflé
		syringe	séringue
hospital	lopital	tears	larme
ill	malad	toothache	léden faire mal
illness	maladi	tranquilizer	tranquilizan
indigestion	indizestion	ulcer	ulcerre
infection	infection	unconscious	perdi connais-sance
infectious	contazié		
inhaler	linhalataire	unwell	pa bien
insect repellent	lotion conte moustic	urgent	irzen
		urinate	pisser
insomnia	linsomni, pa capave dormi	urine	pisar
		vaccination	vaccination
itch	graté/lagratel	virus	viris
malaria	maléria	voice	lavoi
measles	larouzol	vomit	vomi/vomismen
medical certificate	papier doctaire	wart	poro
		weak	faib
medicine	medcine	worm	léver
miscarriage	fos cous	wound	bléshir
mosquito bite	piqué par moustic		
muscle	musc		
nausea	nausé		
nerve	ner		
nose bleed	néné sainnié		
nurse	infirmier/e m/f		
operation	opération		
organ	organ		
pain	doulaire/faire mal		
pain killer	calman		

As can be seen, almost all the vocabulary to do with health is Creolized French. If you cannot remember a word in Creole but know it in French, just say it in that language and you will be understood.

Call an ambulance!	Appel ene lambilance!
Where's the nearest hospital?	Cote lopital pli pré été?
Can I do anything?	Mo capave faire quit soze?
Let me through - I'm a doctor	Laisse mo passer mo ene doctaire
There's been an accident	Ene acciden finn arrivé
I've been stung by a wasp	Ene mous zaune finn pic moi
There are a lot of mosquitoes	Enan boucou moustic
Call a doctor quickly!	Appel ene doctaire vite!
Is there a doctor here?	Esqui énan ene doctaire ici?
My nose is bleeding	Mo néné pé sainnier
She's fainted	Li finn perdi connaissance
He's bleeding profusely	Li pé sainnier boucou
I can't move/walk	Mo pa capave bouzer/marcer
I'm ill/not well	Mo malad/ pa bien
I have a temperature	Mo pé faire lafiève
I've caught a cold	Mo finn enrimé
I've had a fall	Mo finn tombé
I slipped on a babana skin	Mo finn glissé lor lapo banane
My back hurts	Mo lédo/lérin faire mal
He's had a heart attack	Li finn gagne ene attac lécaire
I feel sick	Mo énan malocaire (F. *mal au coeur*)
I want to be sick	Mo envi vomi
She has a heart condition	Li énan malad lécaire
The boy has earache	Garson la énan malad zoreil
My baby has colic	Mo ti baba énan colic
My daughter has broken her glasses	Mo tifi finn cass so linette
Her denture is broken	So fos den finn cassé
I'm in terrible pain	Mo énan doulaire terib
I'm hurt	Mo finn blessé
She needs somewhere to breast-feed her baby	Li bizin quit par pou donne so baba tété
The woman has lost a lot of blood	Sa femme la finn perdi boucou disan
Is she seriously injured?	Esqui li finn blessé terib?
It hurts here	Li faire mal ici
Can you recommend a doctor?	Ou capave recomann ene doctaire?
I need an injection	Mo bizin faire ene piqire
I'm under medication	Mo pé suive traitemen
He's had an epileptic fit	Li finn gagne ene attac épilepsi
I can't eat/drink	Mo pa capave manzé/boire
I'm so thirsty	Mo gagne soif terib
Can I have some water, please?	Ou capave donne moi impé dilo, sivouplé?
I've no appetite	Mo pénan lapéti
I've got diarrhoea	Mo finn gagne diaré

It's a touch of indigestion	**Ene tighin indizestion**
I can't sleep	**Mo pa capave dormi**
I feel sleepy	**Mo gagne someil**
She can't breathe	**Li pa capave respirer**
Is it serious	**Esqui li sérié?**
I think he's dying	**Mo croire li pé mor**
He's only drunk	**Li sou sellemen**
The child is not well	**Zenfan la pa bien**
Will he have to go to hospital?	**Esqui li pou bizin alle lopital?**
I feel much better	**Mo boucou pli bien**
Will I be able to travel?	**Esqui mo pou capave voyazer?**

WARNING

Visitors to Mauritius may be questioned by the police if they are found in possession of tranquillizers and hypnotics such as Valium, Rohypnol, Lexomil, Ativan and other dangerous drugs eg Co-Proxamol tablets.

In order to avoid unnecessary problems, you are advised to take with you a covering prescription and/or a medical certificate to prove that you need these drugs for medicinal purposes. It is always a good idea to carry with you a copy of your latest prescription(s). It is also preferable to keep the drugs in their original containers, with the name and address of the dispensing chemist intact, as it is not uncommon for medicines to be called by different names in other countries. But there should be no difficulty getting the drugs most commonly prescribed in Britain on the island; there are so many pharmacies that they probably outnumber the fast-food outlets.

FLORA AND FAUNA

One bird you cannot escape when in Mauritius is the famous dodo. But alas, being unable to escape itself was the cause of its downfall. This giant, flightless endemic pigeon, was so tame and trusting that it did not escape the Dutch settlers of the 17th century who killed and ate the dodo into extinction.

Tourism has resurrected the dodo and today the bird can be seen on postcards, paintings, T-shirts, company logos, jewellery and in models made of wood, brass or plastic for tourists to take home as souvenirs. Other threatened birds which were heading for extinction but appear to be enjoying a reprieve thanks to the hard work of dedicated foreign ornithologists are: the Mauritius kestrel, the Echo parakeet and the Pink pigeon.

Only the common birds in Mauritius have Creole names. Less common ones are referred to by their common French names and will be known only to Mauritians who are interested in birds. Creole names are given here where known.

ENDEMIC BIRDS

Blackbird	**Merle**
Cuckoo shrike	**Couzinié**
Echo parakeet	**Gro cato ver**
Flycatcher	**Gob mous/coq des bois**
Grey white eye	**Zoizo manioc/ pic pic**
Mauritius fody	**Cardinal, zoizo banane**
Mauritius kestrel	**Crécérel**
Olive white eye	**lizié blan/oiseau à lunette**
Pink pigeon	**Pizon rose/pigeon des mares**

Red-tailed tropic bird	**Paille-en-queue à brins rouges**
Sooty tern	**Yéyé**
Trinidade petrel	**Pétrel de la Trinité**
Wedge-tailed shearwater	**Fouquet**
White-tailed tropic bird	**Payenké/paille-en-queue**

INDIGENOUS LAND BIRDS

Madagascar turtle dove	**Pizon ramier**
Mascarene martin	**Gros hirondelle**

INDIGENOUS OCEANIC BIRDS

Blue faced booby	**Fou**
Brown noddy	**Macoua**

INTRODUCED SPECIES

House sparrow	**moino**	Rock dove	**pizon colombe**
Indian grey francolin	**perdri**	Spice finch	**damier**
Indian house crow	**corbo**	Spotted dove	**gro tourterel**
Madagascar red fody	**cardinal**	Wax bill	**bengali**
Mynah	**martin**	Weaver bird	**sérin dicap**
Red-whiskered bulbul	**condé**	Yellow-fronted canary	**sérin dipéy**
Ring-necked parakeet	**ti cato**	Zebra dove	**ti tourterel**

ANIMALS AND PESTS

Mauritius has very few endemic animals and most of what can still be called 'wild animals', none of which are dangerous, were either originally introduced by the Dutch to provide meat, or are escaped domestic animals, such as pigs, which are now hunted as **cosson maron**. Others were brought to the island by subsequent settlers for various reasons and have since thrived. One example is the mongoose, which was brought from India to control the population of rats but is itself now a nuisance. And there are pests even in paradise! This is an appropriate place to include some creatures that you may encounter. The Creole names are given first as these are what the Mauritians call them.

camaléon	chameleon, really a species of agama from India
canar mani	Muscovy duck, introduced by the French
cancréla	cockroach
carapat	tick
catacatac	grasshopper
cenpat/milpat	centipede
cerf	Java deer (may be killed during the hunting season)
cosson maron	wildboar
coulève	non-poisonous snake from India (rare)
lézar	lizard
liève	hare, from India, hunted all year round. Mesmerized by car headlights at night and provide easy game for curry for some drivers
mangous	mongoose, can be seen darting across the road between sugarcane fields
mootouk	maggot
mous caca	bluebottle
mous dimiel	honey bee
mous zaune	wasp, reputed for their sting!
nik fourmi	ant hill

nik mous dimiel/ zaune	hive nest/wasps' nest
pis	flea
sauve souri	bats - fruit bat and golden bat (indigenous)
tang	tailless, hedgehog-like animal
tenrec/tandrac	a cousin of tang
torti	giant turtle, seen only in public enclosures
zaco	Macaque monkey. Can be seen in Rivière Noire region and blamed for eating kestrels' eggs. Some are domesticated
zanimo	animal (F. *animaux*)

FLORA

The flora of this tiny island is disappearing fast as the little forest that is left is being cleared for sugar cane, housing and hotels. Less than one per cent of the original forest remains to be enjoyed. The trees, plants and flowers that you can still see are listed below.

badamier	Indian almond, a huge tree which provides welcome shade
bougainvil	bougainvillea, grows well all over the island; various colours
éboni	ebony trees were once abundant. According to historians one reason for the Dutch abandoning Mauritius in 1710 was because they had cleared the island of most of its ebony.
fatac	a tall grass used as hedges and for brooms
filao	casuarina tree - provides shade at seaside but don't sit on its cones!
flamboyan/ bouquet banané	the flamboyant tree bursts into bloom in December/January hence its common name - happy new year bouquet
franzipan	frangipani
gandia	local marijuana
gomo	seaweed, moss
gouyave	guava - red: **gouyave décine**; yellow: **gouyave zaune/ défrance**
hibiskis	hibiscus
laliane	banyan tree; its bright red and black seeds are known as **la grain diabe** (devil's seed)
mazambon	aloe vera, grows wild and is used for medicinal purposes
poinsétia	poinsettia
ravinal	traveller's tree, found in woods and on river banks
vacoa	screw pine; its leaves are used to make the ubiquitous **tente** (basket, carrier)

DOMESTIC AND WILD ANIMALS AND BIRDS SEEN IN MAURITIUS

English	Creole	English	Creole
animal	**zanimo**	guinea fowl	**pintad**
bird	**zoizo**	hare	**liève**
bull	**bef**	hen	**poul**
cat	**sat**	horse	**séval/souval**
cockerell	**coq**	monkey	**zaco**
cow	**vas**	peacock	**pan**
deer	**cerf**	pig	**cosson**
dog	**licien**	pigeon	**pizon**
donkey	**bouric**	rabbit	**lapin**
duck	**canar**	sheep	**mouton**
goat	**cabri**	tortoise	**torti**
goose	**lézoi**	turkey	**dinde**

MISCELLANEOUS

WEIGHTS AND MEASURES AND SEMI-TECHNICAL WORDS

depth	**profonderre**	round	**ron**
flat	**platte**	square	**caré**
heavy	**lour**	thick	**épai**
height	**hoterre**	thickness	**épaisserre**
length	**longuerre**	thin	**mince**
light	**lézé**	weight	**poi**
measure	**mésire**	width	**larzerre**

acre	**arpen**	hectare	**hectar**
amp	**ampaire**	inch	**pouce**
area	**granderre**	kilogram	**kilo**
centimetre	**centimette**	litre	**litte**
diameter	**diamette**	metre	**mette**
foot	**pied**	milimetre	**milimette**
furlong	**ferlong**	ounce	**once**
gallon	**galon**	pound	**liv**
gram	**gram**	volt	**vot**

whole	**entié**	three quarters	**troi car**
half	**lamoitié, edmi**	one-third	**ene tierre**
quarter	**ene car**	equal	**égal**

OLD FRENCH MEASURES STILL IN USE

arpen	about an acre
arpenterre	surveyor
perche	100th part of an arpent, pronounced **perse**
toise	approximately six French feet
toise carré	an area equivalent to 36 French square feet

TOOLS

blunt	**pa fité**	screw	**vis**
chisel	**cizo/cizo froi**	screw driver	**tournavis**
drill	**mes**	sharp	**fité**
hammer	**marto**	step ladder	**lésel, escabo**
nail	**coulou**	paint	**lapeintire**
plane	**rabo**	paint brush	**pinso**
pliers/pincers	**tanaille**	penknife	**canif**
saw	**larsar**	tape measure	**mette riban**

HOUSING TERMS

balcony	**balcon**	roof tile	**tuilt**
bathroom	**lasalbain**	room	**lasam**
bedroom	**lasam dormi**	staircase	**lescalier**
door	**laporte**	steps	**péron**
glasspane	**vite**	storey	**létaze**
kitchen	**lacouzine**	toilet	**drainaze, cabinet**
larder/pantry	**garde manzé**	veranda	**lavarang**
loft	**grénié**	wall	**mirail**
lounge	**salon**	window	**lafénette**
roof	**toi**	yard	**lacour**

OTHER CREOLE TERMS

baliécoco/fatac	local broom made of the stems of coconut leaves/tall grass
bis/ter	seen in house numbering: 2A = 2bis, 3B = 3ter
campemen	seaside villa/bungalow
cité	housing estate
godon	small room leading to the veranda
lacaze	house, any dwelling place or home. Eg **lacaze lamort** - mortuary; **lacaze laraigner** - spider's web; **lacaze zoizo** - bird cage
lacorde coco	local rope made of coconut fibre
lapaille coco	coconut fibre used to stuff mattresses etc
morcelmen	parcelling/dividing of land into small lots; a housing estate
rotin bazar	cane: used in school for caning; for furniture making
pirog	small wooden fishing boat with mast and sails
také	1. catch, latch, any door fastener; 2. light switch
tente	local carrier bags made of vacoa (screw pine) leaves

ABOUT THE HOUSE

bed	**lili** (F. *le lit*)	nail brush	**bros zong**
broom	**balié**		(F *ongle*)
brush	**bros**	nail clipper	**tail zong**
chair	**sèze**	needle and thread	**zégui ek difil**
clock	**réveil**	night light	**véyez**
couch	**sofa**	power point/plug	**prize**
curtain	**rido**	record player	**tournedis**
dishwasher	**macine lave**	scales	**balance**
	vaiselle	scissors	**cizo**
doormat	**payason**	sewing machine	**macine acoud**
dressing table	**coifèze**	shelf	**létazer**
floor	**plancer, parquet**	shower	**dous**
fridge	**frizidaire**	table	**latab**
iron	**ferre, caro**	toilet soap	**savonet**
lampshade	**labazour/abazour**	toothbrush	**bros a den**
light bulb	**globe**	toothpaste	**dentifrice**
light switch	**také**	towel	**serviette**
meter: electric/	**conterre: électric/**	vacuum cleaner	**aspirataire,hoover**
water	**dilo**	wardrobe	**larmoire**
mirror	**miroir, laglace**	washing machine	**macine a laver**

THE OFFICE

adhesive tape	**sélotep™**	letter	**let**
cash box	**boite lacaisse**	letter opener	**coupe papier**
desk	**bireau, latab**	letter paper	**papier a let**
directory	**lannière**	paper clip	**tronbonne**
envelope	**lenvlop**	pen	**plime**
fax	**télécopi, fax**	pencil sharpener	**fitoire**
fax machine	**télécopierre**	receipt	**réci**
filing cabinet	**claserre**	rubber stamp	**tampon, estampe**
invoice	**factire**	typewriter	**macine a écrire**

Most modern office electronic equipment has no Creole equivalent, instead the English names are used. Eg computer, scanner.

PUBLIC NOTICES

Official notices are in English and French and published or displayed side by side. Other private or public notices and signs may be in either English or French. The following are some common ones which are self-explanatory.

Beware of the dog	*Attention chien méchant*
Car park	*Parking*
Entrance	*Entrée*
For sale	*A vendre*
No admittance	*Défense d'entrer*
No parking	*Interdiction de se garer*
No smoking	*Défense de fumer*
Notice	*Avis*
Taxis only	*Réservé aux taxis*

RELIGIOUS FESTIVALS AND ANNIVERSARIES*

CHRISTIAN

All Saints	**Latousain**
Ascension Day	**Lasension**
Ash Wednesday	**Mercredi désanne**
Assumption of the Virgin	**Fète de la Vierze**
Christmas	**Noel**
Corpus Christi	**Fète dé Dié**
Easter	**Pac**
Epiphany	**Lépifani**
Good Friday	**Vendredi Sain**
Palm Sunday	**Fète dé ramo**
Trinity Sunday	**Fète dé la Trinité**
Whit Sunday	**Lapentecote**

HINDU

Diwali	**Divali**
Holi	**Holi**
Maha Shivaratri	**Maha Sivrati**
Navrati	**Navaratri**
New year	**Nav varsh**

Ougadi	**Ougadi**
Thaipoosam	**Cavadee**
Cavadee	

ISLAMIC

Eid-Ul-Fitr	**Id**
Eid-Al-Adha	**Bacarid**
Ramadhan	**Ramadan, careme**

CHINESE

Spring Festival/ New Year	**Lanné sinois**

Several other religious festivals, not listed here, are also celebrated in Mauritius.

63

MUSICAL TERMS

bal bobesse
former informal dancing party practised by Creoles in villages

bal rande zarico
a party at which a cake containing a bean is cut up and served. The person getting the slice of cake with the bean has to give the next party

baré
during a sega dance, a male dancer opens his arm wide as if to prevent his partner from escaping

bob/bobre
a crude musical instrument with a single string resembling an archer's bow and using half a calabash as a sound box

cass lérin
wriggling of the hip during dancing

catia catia
a percussion instrument, usually a coconut shell with seeds, which is shaken

cayembé
a bamboo percussion instrument

eh-la-eh-la-eh!
the ségatier's signal for everyone to join in a sega dance

enba! enba!
what the man says in a sega dance as he gradually crouches down, inviting his partner to do the same

kélélé
that stage in a sega dance when the male dancer makes a gesture as if offering his body to his partner

maravanne
a rectangular box containing seeds, now a traditional sega musical instrument

mootia
an old, rustic variety of sega

morion
a kind of drum

noir mootia
a person who used to like dancing the old version sega

ravanne
the basic, most important musical instrument of sega - a simple drum. Now a traditional instrument

sega
the folk-dance of Mauritius. This term is used to describe the dance rhythm, the dance, as well as the music, whether played or sung. See chapter *The History of Mauritius and its Languages - Whither Creole?*

ségatier
a composer/singer/ and/or performer of sega

tabla (l)
a small drum

terre a terre
the most sexually suggestive movement in sega dance, known as the 'copulating position'. As the couple crouch, the woman leans over backwards and her partner extends his body over hers and the position is reversed and repeated several times during a dance

triang
a musical triangle, the source of the tinkling sound heard above the beat of the **ravanne** in a sega. The **triang**, **ravanne** and the **maravanne** were the basic instruments used in traditional sega (**séga typique**)

Surf to Mauritius

Visit our website to find out more about Mauritius

General Information
Facts and figures; History; Current news

Language and Culture
Creole - the language of Mauritius; Sega - the Mauritian folkdance; Mauritian cuisine

Visiting Mauritius
Travel agencies; Places to visit; Mauritius - Information Pack; What they say about Mauritius

Books and Reviews
Books about Mauritius; Rare books; Latest reviews;

More about Mauritius
The government; The economy

Mauritians Abroad
Mauritian International magazine; Directory of Mauritian Businesses in the UK; Society of Mauritian Artists and Writers; Speakers on Mauritius

www.mauritiusworld.com

PART TWO

CRAZY CREOLE

As mentioned earlier, Mauritian Creole has no rules, so anything goes. Consequently the language now contains some phrases whose literal translations are simply 'crazy' to non-Mauritians. This is particularly so where a French word has acquired a Creole meaning, such as the word *casser* (to break). *Gagner* is another word which in Creole is used more in the sense of to get or to be, rather than its French meaning of to gain, to earn or to win. Below are a few examples.

Alle enba la rivierre - rather difficult to do. Literally it means go underneath the river. In Mauritius it signifies by the riverside.

Allez right - wrong! It does not mean "go right" but okay, fine.

Arab – not a Middle Easterner, not in Creole. It is a term still used by some islanders to refer to Mauritians of Muslim faith. Strangely enough, although there is no Arab population in Mauritius and only a few Arabs in transit, there is an Arab Town in Rose Hill.

Are – in crazy Creole the plural of 'is' means 'with' or 'together with'. Eg **Li are nou** means "s/he is with us".

Boite condané - a person whose mother tongue is not English would not be able to tell what 'piggy bank' was from the words. It is not a bank for pigs nor, as in 'blood bank', a place where pigs are kept. Literally **boite condané** means a condemned box, a box locked up in jail. Being crazy Creole it is not the box that is condemned but the coins children put into it. It is an appropriate description of a child's money box.

Byedoom - not goodbye, you're doomed! It is the name given to the people Mauritians try to avoid – those who used to empty latrines. They were usually prisoners on forced labour, as no-one else would do the job.

Cap lécol - playing truant. Not a school cap or one on a cape, as in headland.

Cass contour - break the corner. Another way of saying turn a corner.

Cass fes - to steal. Its literal meaning of "breaking your buttocks" may lead English-speaking people to assume it means to pinch one's bottom. It requires some imagination to see the connection with stealing when **cassaire fes** means a shameless, dishonest person. Literally - someone who goes about kicking people's posteriors.

Cass palto - break the jacket. The origin of this is a mystery, as it means a very strong alcoholic drink. Maybe you may have to take off your jacket after drinking it as you'll feel warm.

Cass paquet - break the packet. No parcel is involved! It means to be on to a good thing, to take full advantage of an opportunity. It can also mean to make love. **A nou cass paquet** roughly translates as let's get cracking.

Cass paquet diboi - break the bundle of wood. Why this term should be used to refer to a handshake may be to do with what is known as a "grip of steel". Those on the receiving end feel that their fingers are a bunch of matchsticks being squeezed to breaking point!

Fancy-fair – pronounced **fennecy ferre**. It does not mean a fancy dress do, so don't turn up in a clown costume. It is just a name for a fund-raising event, usually a church fête.

Faire titour - if a Mauritian male says this to you, he is not going for a little tour, its literal meaning, but probably to find a tree trunk or secluded wall against which to relieve himself.

Gagne baté - to be defeated (in a game). Literally: to gain defeat. Even in losing the Mauritians 'gain'!

Gagne bon - not to gain goodness but to experience (sexual) pleasure.

Gagne dimal/doulaire - to suffer pain.

Gagne faim - to be/feel hungry.

Gagne frai - to be/feel cold.

Gagne lahonte - to feel ashamed.

Gagne panne - broken down, usually refers to a machine. Eg **Mo loto finn gagne panne** (my car has broken down). An alternative is **mo loto finn tombe en panne** (literally: my car has fallen broken down).

Gagne pied - not to gain a foot but probably connected with "give him an inch and he takes a foot". It means to take liberties.

Gagne someil - to be/feel sleepy.

Gagne zaffaire - not to have an affair but to have dealings with someone.

Lave latète - hair wash. Perhaps it makes sense if you're doing so in a shower. Literally: head wash.

Manze difé - literally to eat fire but it means to drink excessively; an inveterate drinker.

Nam - soul, ghost. Also used to describe someone who is passionate about something, eg **li ene nam football** (he is football-mad). This is an example of Creolisation of the French *âme* with a change in meaning.

Pété dinde - literally: turkey hen farts! Freckles. According to the Mauritians a person with a freckled face must have been unfortunate enough to be in the wrong place when a turkey was 'unwinding'. It shows the imaginative and colourful provenance of Mauritian expressions.

Pié - the horticultural meaning of this word is more wide-ranging in Creole: it is not restricted to a small plant but applies to all trees of any size. After all, a tree is a tree is a tree.

Sapé - the crazy Creole version of the French verb *échapper*. It is not just the word that has changed, but its meaning too, from "to get away from" to "to be lucky". Eg **Li sapé dilo la pa bouyante** (he/she is lucky the water is not boiling hot).

Saute lari - cross the road. Literally it means jump the road - it must be so dangerous that walking across the road is not fast enough! You may even hear **saute vite!** (jump quickly!) when people are crossing the road.

Sof soleil - literally: warm the sun - an impossibility! It means sunning oneself, as chameleons do.

So latète finn dépasse so cévé - the closest English equivalent may be "too big for his boots". Literally: his head has outgrown his hair.

Tigit - not a small git but a small quantity.

CRAZY NUMBERS

A numerical slang has long existed in Mauritius. Some examples are:

- 1 - expert, ace
- 2 - monkey
- 3 - ear
- 4 - death
- 5 - Muslim
- 6 - homosexual man
- 7 - thief
- 8 - octopus
- 9 - never
- 11 - feet
- 14 - crazy
- 15 - breasts
- 17 - girlfriend
- 20 - to run
- 21 - drunkard
- 22 - shoes
- 24 - food, (also a very small hook)
- 27 - policeman
- 28 - go off the rails/ to escape
- 29 - to urinate
- 31 - pensioner
- 32 - Chinese
- 33 - child
- 34 - clever
- 35 - mistress - *girlfriend*
- 36 - black
- 40 - arse, bum

A conversation using numerical slang may go something like this: **"Ene 27 et so 17 pé faire galan quand zotte trouve ene 7 pé 20. Li trappe li facilmen parcequi li ene 21 san 22."** (A policeman and his girlfriend were courting when they saw a thief running away. The policeman caught the thief easily because he was a drunkard without any shoes on).

If you are a 34 33 and have not 28, and you still have not got the gist of it by now, you 9 will!

The missing numbers mean there is no consistency regarding their meanings. As can be seen, numbers 24 and 28 are used to indicate two different things in each case. They are listed here as both are quite well known.

CREOLE RHYMES

Nursery rhymes and lullabies have also evolved in the vernacular. Here follow some better-known ones which most Mauritian children must have sung, or recited at home or at play. The Creole is more French than that spoken everyday and shows their French origin.

Zacana

Qui ti teigne mon fé?
Zène sai pa
Zacana! Zacana!
Bé bé
To piti pou moi
Et to menti
A nou parier
Sé qui to ou lé
Si mo gagne li
Mo faire bouyon
Ah, si mo gagne li
Mo faire bouyon
Ah, si mo gagne li
Mo faire bouyon

Larivierre Tanier

Mo passer larivierre Tanier
Mo zoinne ene vié bonnefemme
Mo dire li qui li faire la
Li dire moi lapes cabo
Mo donne li ene moussoir disic
Li donne moi ene moussoir cabo
Oui, oui mes zenfan
Il faut travailler pour avoir son pain

Untitled

Qui passer la?
Marsan dilait
Qui dilait?
Dilait cayé
Qui cayé?
Cahier dévoir
Qui dévoir?

Dévoir anglé
Qui Anglé?
Anglé potis
Qui potis?
Potis zasar
Qui zasar?
Zasar mang
Qui mang?
Mang lacorde
Qui lacorde?
Lacorde coco
Qui coco?
Coco manzé
Qui manzé?
Manzé cosson
Qui cosson?
Cosson dan parc
Qui parc?
Parc diboi
Qui diboi?
Diboi colofanne
Si mo gagne li
Cen coute baton

CREOLE IDIOMS, INTERJECTIONS AND SLANG EXPRESSIONS

This chapter will appeal to readers who have an interest in language. It contains Creole terms, phrases and interjections that are unique to this language. Although many of them originated in French, the connection is no longer always apparent. Over the centuries they have evolved into expressions that only Mauritians seem able to understand. They are the most difficult part of the language to translate or explain to foreigners.

Hopefully the explanations supplied (with literal translations where appropriate) will help readers to get a flavour of Mauritian Creole; an understanding of such terms will certainly give a new dimension to your holiday. A foreigner who is able to use any of these expressions in conversation with Mauritians will impress them no end! You may even come to like the language.

In this chapter you will also find other Creole words or terms that do not quite fit into any other sections.

Aiyaya! - an interjection you will hear a lot in conversations expressing disappointment (of Chinese origin?)
Agram bagram - doing things in a disorderly fashion; in a mess (Indian)
Arranze so carri - to punish someone (to sort out their dish/food)
Ayo! - Oh dear! Ouch! Also surprise, sorrow (I)
Balier caro - winning the lottery jackpot, winning convincingly (sweep the field)
Baplé bap - an expression of shock, surprise; an exclamation of hopelessness (still in transition from Indian to Creole)
Bato pancor (F. *pas encore*) **débarquer** - this refers to a woman who is in the final stage of pregnancy (the ship has not landed yet)
Baton papaye - anything weak, easily breakable (pawpaw's tree trunk breaks easily)
Batte caca faire mastic - trying to do the impossible (to beat faeces into putty)
Batte dilo pou gagne lavie - fishing illegally (beat water to make a living)
Batte ene caré - a short walk/stroll (to knock out a square)
Batte lamoc - a failure (concert, show etc), hardly any audience (beat an empty tin can)
Batte lézelle - said of someone who is beginning to gain self-confidence (to flap their wings)
Bèf dan disab, sacaine guette so lizié - everyone for himself (the cattle are in the sand, they look into each other's eyes)
Bez/bézé - annoyance
Bézerre (Creole?) **paquet** - a despicable person (a wicked bundle)
Bona vini - any old how (F. *bonne venue*)
Caca enplace - to be seized with great fear/pain (to defecate on the spot)
Caleson-sémize - inseparable friends (trousers and shirt)
Caraille (I) **so** - short of money (the frying pan is hot)
Caro canne finn pren difé - a sarcastic remark made to anyone who has had a very

short haircut (the cane field has caught fire)

Cass/casser - to break (F) has several meanings in Creole, eg to pick flowers, change money into smaller denominations, to deflower

Cass caca lizié - to pick discharge off one's eyes, to rub one's eyes on awakening (to break up eyes' faeces)

Cass-casser - in bad condition (broken-broken)

Cass coaltar - to drive very fast (breaking the asphalt)

Cass coco - to knock two heads together (to break open a coconut)

Cass cou - to nod off (to break a moment)

Cass lélan - to lose momentum (to break momentum)

Cass lizié - to dazzle (to damage the eyes)

Cass ménaze - to lure a spouse away (to break up a home)

Cass paquet - to get cracking; to make love (to break the packet [of a condom?])

Cass paquet diboi - to shake hands (to untie a bundle of wood)

Cass pares - to stretch oneself (to break laziness)

Cass pause - to take a rest (to break a pause)

Cass pican - to run away very fast (to trample on thorns)

Cass so laguel - to beat someone up (to smash their face)

Cass sommeil - to wake up (to break sleep)

Casserre fes - a cheat, double-dealer (an arse-breaker)

Cass, Ene sou ene - a little money (a cent, two cents - **cas/s** is a two-cent coin, **sou** is the smallest denomination coin)

Cass, Pa cass latète - don't worry (don't break your head)

Cause to (zot - plural) **cauzé** - talk about/discuss your affairs (talk your talk)

Cause couyon - a telling off

Cause traverre - to talk in metaphore (to speak crooked)

Cause madame séré - a form of pig Latin or back slang; a kind of secret language incomprehensible to the uninitiated. Each syllable is repeated, and other rules apply, eg where a syllable begins with a vowel, g may be added and so on. The use of **langaze madame séré** may be heard, say, on a public beach, spoken by a group of young men who do not want the other sunbathers to understand what they are saying to each other. Eg "are there any topless women on the beach? " in Creole is **esqui énan fem touni lor laplaze?** Translated into **madame séré** it becomes **es es qui qui e e nan nan fem fem tou tou ni ni lor lor la la plaze plaze?**

Coco long - bald (long forehead)

Costé - near, come nearer (F. *accoster)*

Cote to finn sapé? (F. *échapper) -* where have you sprung from? (where have you escaped from?)

Coulou sispouce - a tall person (six-inch nail)

Coume sa mem Maurice/Li coume sa Maurice - a stock answer to any complaint about Mauritius (that's how it is in Mauritius)

Cou doub - double success (at horse races)

Cou sec - to drink a tot of rum (or spirits) in one gulp (dry hit)

Crazaire (F. *écraser*) **dizef** - a bully (an egg breaker)

74

Craze ene séga - let's sing a sega
Craze lérin - to run as fast as possible (to break the kidneys)
Craze mil - to walk a long distance (to pound the miles)
Craze terrain - to run away fast (to pound the ground)
Dan gout - very appealing/attractive (in taste)
Dan laclé - in trouble (in the key); probably intended to mean inside a lock
Déminit cat - in a trice (2.4 minutes)
Dessane (F. *descendre*) **lor pied** - pay the bill, settle one's debts (come down from the tree top)
Dessane so caleson - to make someone give in (to pull down someone's trousers)
Dilo dormi - stagnant water (sleeping water)
Doctaire poul - a quack doctor (a hen doctor)
Douk - bad luck; **en douk** - in distress/trouble
Enba laho - upside down (under above)
Ene niméro - a nuisance (F. *un numéro*)
Ene tipimen - a cheeky child; a naughty, devilish woman (a small chilli)
Envil - in town/to the town (this term is used only to refer to Port Louis, the capital, eg **Mo alle envil** - I'm going to Port Louis)
Età/étahé! - interjection to express disbelief or regret, only used between friends

The verb **faire** (to do, to make) is used at the beginning of many sentences, instructions, exclamations and so on as an all-encompassing, useful word:
Faire cinquième larou - to become/act as a substitute (to make a fifth wheel)
Faire coco - to embrace, cuddle (**coco** here means head - to bring heads together)
Faire comeraze - to do something unnecessary, not supposed to
Faire commerre - women's gossip
Faire disan marce dan lécor - to provoke one's anger, indignation (to make blood walk within the body)
Faire dominaire - to bully , to ill-treat someone (to dominate)
Faire ene caré - go for a short walk (to do a square)
Faire érerre - to cheat, do wrong (to make an error)
Faire foute - don't give a damn (F.*va te faire foutre*)
Faire gran noir - to put on airs (to act like a big important black person)
Faire gran tour - to defecate (to make a grand tour - see **faire titour**)
Faire lafemme - to behave like a woman/be effeminate. Usually in the negative: **pa faire lafemme** - don't behave like a woman (to be a woman)
Faire latète lipied - to do everything possible (to do head to feet)
Faire létalaze - to overdo things, to do more than necessary
Faire li danser - to punish someone, to force a person to pay up (to make him dance
Faire lipou poul - to be long-winded (to make chicken nits)
Faire lizié dou - to make eyes at someone (to make sweet eyes)
Faire macro - to grass, tell on someone (to pimp)
Faire martin - to tell on someone, to gossip about news best kept to oneself (to be like the bird, the martin)
Faire Pac avan carem -to have sex before marriage (to celebrate Easter before Lent)

Faire regardan - to be fussy, finicky
Faire tis - to urinate (to make urine)
Faire titour (F.*petit tour*) - to go for a pee (to go for a stroll)
Faire vantar - to show off
Faire zaco - to make faces (to be a monkey)
Faire zes (F.*geste*) - showing off, putting on an act (to make gestures)
Foul - full; **ene foul suppoterre** - a solid supporter
Gagne baté - to be defeated in a game, to be beaten up (to gain a defeat)
Gagne bézé - to be badly defeated in a game; a set-back
Gagne bon - to experience (sexual) pleasure
Gagne délicat - to feel a distaste, aversion to certain food (to gain delicate)
Gagne granderre - to assume importance (to gain height, greatness)
Gagne lagam - to get into the mood
Gagne ner - nervy, to be on edge
Garde dan lécaire - to bear a grudge (to keep in the heart)
Gaté pourri - spoilt rotten
Gatte latète - to put bad ideas/thoughts into someone's head (to ruin the head)
Golmal - untidy (I)
Gran dilo - a loose woman (a lot of water)
Gran dimoune - an important person
Gran/gro palto - a big shot (big jacket)
Gran laguel - a loud-mouthed person
Gran lespri/lespri ouver - a broad-minded person (big minded/open minded)
Gran noir - a person who has achieved important economic status (big black person)
Gratte lamer peintir léciel - to do unnecessary work (scrape the sea, paint the sky)
Gro boudouf (Creole?) - a fat person
Guette dé lizié - to have double standards about someone's work (to see with two eyes)
Guette en ba lizié - to scowl at someone (to see from under the eyes)
Guette traverre - to look at someone in anger, to be cross with someone (to look at crookedly)
Labous cabri - a spiteful person (a goat's mouth)
Labous graté - to say things likely to offend (itchy mouth)
Labous mofinne (Portuguese) - a person whose words bring bad luck (bad luck mouth)
Lafièvre carante - high fever, with a temperature of 40 degrees
Lalang bien fité - a sharp tongue
Lamain/lamé enba ros - to have one's hands tied (hand underneath a rock)
Lamé diboi - a bad driver (wooden hand)
Lamé larze - a big spender (large hand)
Lamé long - a kleptomaniac (long hand)
Lamé lour - a miser (heavy hand)
Lamé zouzoute (Creole) - a person with poor dexterity
Largue lamé - to learn a trade, a skill (to loosen the hand)
Largue lavoi - to speak out (to release the voice)

Largue lécor - to give up (to give up the body)
Largue so lécourse - to chase away (to start his/her race)
Las de pic - parson's nose (ace of spades)
Laserpe - cane chopper
La tète camaron (Portuguese)/**cocom** - a head like a sieve, said of a person who is forgetful (prawn/cucumber head)
La tète fromaze - a bald person (cheese head)
Letan mangoze - a long time ago
Leve dormi - to wake up (to wake sleep)
Leve néné (F.*nez*) - to show disapproval (lift one's nose)
Leve mo cadave - to get up from sleep with difficulty, be reluctant to get up (to wake my cadaver)
Leve paquet - to move house (to lift the parcel)
Lindi cordonier - Monday, a day of high absenteeism from work in Mauritius (shoemaker's Monday)
Linze dimance/linze sorti - Sunday best/best clothes (going out clothes)
Lipou poul - a fussy person (chicken louse)
Lizié bigorno - small eyes (winkle eyes)
Lizié boutonierre - slit eyes (buttonhole eyes)
Lor caisse/lor lapail - broke, no money (on the wooden box/on straw)
Macadam - stone chippings (E. MacAdam)
Madame zenlui - a woman who spreads false or ill-natured gossip
Mama poul - a madam of a brothel (mother hen)
Manze banane dan dé boute - to burn the candle at both ends (to eat a banana at both ends)
Manze banane ver - having sex with your future spouse before marriage; to taste the forbidden fruit (to eat a green banana)
Manze féyaze - to bite the dust (to eat foliage)
Manze laqué sat - to speak in a hoarse voice; loss of voice; a frog in one's throat (to have eaten a cat's tail)
Manze so cou - to accept an injustice without protest (to eat blows)
Manze zarico - to be pregnant, a bun in the oven (to have eaten a bean)
Maré graté - at very low tide (the tide is scraping)
Mari conten - most happy. The French word for husband, *mari,* has acquired several new meanings as a superlative: biggest, greatest, loudest, prettiest, most horrible etc. For example: **ene mari match** - a great match; **ene mari carri** - a very good curry
Mariaze en ba bol - an elopement, a secret wedding without guests (wedding under a bowl)
Mariaze lisien - a bitch in heat being followed by several dogs (dog wedding)
Mette dan boite/laclé - to put someone in a difficult position, to hoax someone (to put someone in a box/in a lock)
Mette difé - to put pressure on someone (to set alight)
Mo fes cassé - I'm knackered (my buttocks are beaten)
Mo gaté pourri - my lovely one, my spoilt one (my spoilt rotten)

Monte cadak/cadadak - to ride pick-a-back

Mo plein - I'm full up

Mo plein are li - I'm fed up with him/her

Nam (F.*l'âme*) - a fanatic, an enthusiast (soul)

Niméro ene - top, best, a specialist (number one). See *Crazy numbers*

Noir touni - a pauper (a naked black person)

Nom gaté - nickname (spoiled name)

Ouf! - phew!

Papa! - an interjection expressing surprise

Pa dire moi! - you don't say!

Pa mo carri - I don't fancy it/him/her (not my dish)

Pa rente dan caless cassé - don't get involved with other people's problems (don't go into a broken carriage)

Pa tou létan fète zaco - you can't be lucky everytime (not a monkey's feast every time)

Pass balier - to sweep (the most literal translation for the word **pass** in this context is to circulate, to move - to move the broom)

Pass bros - to brush [the floor] (to move the brush)

Pass caro - to iron (to move the iron)

Pass en ba couto - to have an operation (to go under the knife)

Pass martir - to endure great suffering/poverty (to undergo martyrdom)

Pass miserre - to suffer hardship

Pass par lafénet - 1. Said of a person who bears no resemblance to his father, especially his complexion. This is usually said in jest. An old joke in Mauritius goes: When a baby is born, people don't ask "It is a boy or a girl?" but "What colour is it?" 2. Said of someone who got their job through personal connections (gone in through the window)

Pass sifon - to clean, polish, dust (to move the duster)

Paye lepoc cassé - to be blamed for someone else's wrongdoing. Although **lepoc** also means epoch, here it refers to F. *les pots cassés* - pay for the broken pots

Pété dinde - freckles (turkey's fart)

Pézé néné boire diluile - having to accept something, without choice (pinch your nose, drink the castor oil)

Pi - to lose in gambling or games

Pié douri (F. *du riz*) - the hand that feeds (rice plant)

Pilingué (Bantu) - to have a useless argument

Piok - to lose everything in gambling.

Pioner - to watch discreetly

Piso (F. *puceau*) - said of a team which has not scored any goals/points. It was used in 1982 by newspapers to describe the general election results, in which the ruling alliance did not win a single seat

Plok - 1.a goner, extreme exhaustion; 2. testicles (E. bollocks?)

Ravinal - the traveller's tree (Malagasy)

Right - a tick, as in homework to show it is correct

Ris so laqué - to pull someone's leg, to tease (to pull someone's tail)

Rode lavie - to look for a living (to search where there is life). **Gagne lavie** - to make a living

Ros laver - stone on which clothes are washed

Sati - a devoted wife (I)

Saute la fénette - said of a woman whose child is not fathered by her husband (jump through the window)

Saute lari - cross the road (jump the road)

Sauté pilé - cry of triumph at sports

Ségatier - a composer/singer/dancer of sega, the Mauritian folkdance/music

Sétaki (F. c'est à qui) - each and every

Soze (F.*chose*) - thing, whatsit. Another all-encompassing Creole word which may be used in place of any adjective, noun, verb or adverb which the speaker cannot remember: eg **Cote soze été?** - where is whatitsname?; **Mo finn zoinne soze** - I met you-know-who, **ala ene fim ...soze!** - what a - er -whatsit film!

Stopgo - traffic lights

Tabardene - a term used to describe a noisy, happy-go-lucky person. After Jean-Baptiste Tabardin, a Creole adventurer who sailed the world in the 19th century. Later **ene tabardene** also came to mean a quarrelsome woman. This is a Creole word which was heading for obsolescence but may be given a new lease of life following the publication of Tabardin's memoirs *La vie ou les aventures de J. B Tabardin dans ses voyages*

Tamasa - loosely this means fun, entertainment. Eg "you must come to our dance/party/show, there will be **tamasa**." There used to be a cheap, local and popular wine called **Tamasa**

Tapaire - a street bully; someone who has a reputation for being a hoodlum or a thug.

Tapé! - a very distant version of "You've hit the nail on the head". It is equivalent to "well done!", "fantastic!" which applauds an achievement. It can also mean to bang into, eg **dé camion finn tapé** (two lorries have collided)

Tap lamé - to clap (hit the hands)

Tap lédo - to congratulate someone by clapping them on the back (hit the back)

Tas are li - to stick with someone

Tas dan mémoir - unforgettable (stuck in memory)

Ti dimoune - the disadvantaged (little people)

Ti drink - a short drink (a little drink)

Tifek - have just (a combination of predicate markers) **Mo tifek manzé** - I have just eaten

Ti lécaire (F. *le coeur*) - timid person (little heart)

Ti calité - a small person (small kind)

Timini (Creole?) - a bow tie

Tiombo (F. *tiens bon*) - hold tight

Tiptop- a minibus, usually providing a shuttle service. Originally the name of a bus company providing a minibus service in the capital

Toké -a crazy person, of unsound mind

Tombe dan laboisson - to become an alcoholic (to fall into the drink)

Tombe dan panier - to fall into a trap (to fall into the basket)

Tombe déhor - come outside, a challenge to sort it out outside (to fall outside)

Tombe sec - to faint (to fall neat)

Vand (F. *vendre*) **fes** - to prostitute oneself (to sell one's buttocks)

Vié lapo/siko - an old person (old skin)

Viézenne - a middle-aged bachelor (old young)

Zanfoot (F. *jean-foutre*) - one who dislikes lending his/her things

Zazer (F. *jaseur*) - a chatterbox

Zenfan lacaze - a frequent visitor, considered as one of the family (child of the home)

Zega - a girlfriend

Zougaderre - a gambler

A TASTE OF MAURITIUS

MAURITIAN GASTRONOMY

Most of the dishes, sweets, cakes and other food found in Mauritius have been brought to the island by the various ethnic groups who now live on the island. Over the years, the way of preparing and cooking them, the addition of new ingredients, especially spices and other seasonings, have made them more exotic. In some cases traditional ethnic dishes have evolved into different dishes altogether - they have become Mauritianized or Creolized. For instance, the typical Mauritian **dhal puri** is nothing like the pancake of the same name served in an Indian restaurant in London. Nor are the **chow minn** or **minn frire** (fried noodles) prepared the same way as by Chinese cooks in San Francisco.

Then there have been 'marriages' of these distinct culinary dishes which have resulted in unique Mauritian *pièces de résistance* such as **vindaye** and **rougaille**. The islanders have also developed their own pickles and chutneys, thus providing several side dishes without which a Mauritian meal is not complete.

Finally there are Mauritian **gajak** - snacks and cakes of all sorts and flavours, the most popular being the savoury ones, that are found on sale at almost every street corner and which the islanders expect to be served at any function or gathering. Visitors will soon find that Mauritians are a nation of food lovers who eat all day, often on the hoof; on the way to work, going home from school, on the beach, at the races, in the cinema, or at a game of football.

Because Mauritians are such gourmets and prepare their food with such refinement and to such a high standard, the island has acquired a reputation for its cuisine. This is made up of three of the world's greatest culinary traditions, which it has inherited: Chinese, French and Indian. One travel writer has described Mauritius as "the best place to eat seafood south of Hong Kong." And because a large number of Mauritians are vegetarian for religious reasons, vegetarian dishes abound.

Today the island's cuisine reflects its people, producing exotic dishes made up of these three great cuisines. You may recognise the names of many of the dishes appearing on a menu, but they may not necessarily be prepared in the same traditional way as in their countries of origin. The result is a different taste, giving a wider culinary experience. For example, the Creole *salade de pomme de terre* may have been French in origin, but you will find nothing quite like it in a Parisian restaurant. Similarly *bouillabaisse*, cooked Chinese style with ginger, pepper, tomatoes, coriander, thyme and green chilli, is nothing like the fish soup of Marseille.

The 'Creole cuisine' promoted by the tourist industry is the food that is eaten by most Mauritians irrespective of their ethnic origin (with the exception of older, foreign-born Indians and Chinese) and consists of: curry, **rougaille,** pulses, stewed vegetable leaves, a clear soup or broth made from edible leaves and a salad of cucumber, lettuce or green fruit.

Below is a selection of the commoner dishes, snacks and refreshments that have now become Mauritian, and which a visitor is likely to be offered or to encounter. Try avoiding some of the islanders' favourites! They are to be found everywhere, from being sold by vendors at roadsides, or from bicycles, to the most expensive restaurants and hotels. As they have retained their original ethnic names they have probably contributed the largest number of foreign words to Creole in the last few decades. Visitors will soon realise that Mauritians prefer savoury food, but there are also a lot of sweet cakes and confectionery, which is not surprising since the country produces over 700,000 tonnes of sugar per year.

Alouda - a typical, refreshing, iced sweet drink sold in markets and at open-air events. Non-alcoholic, and with different flavourings. Its essential ingredient is **tookmaria** seeds, which swell up in water into slippery, gelatinous balls that float like tadpoles in the drink. A great favourite in hot weather. Varieties include with milk, with chopped jelly etc.

Baja - roundish savoury fried snack, sold piping hot by street vendors and at **lotel dité**. Made of flour, usually gram, with chopped spring onion, chilli and other spices. Two versions: **gro baja** and **ti baja** (I).

Biscui manioc - this unique biscuit is as Mauritian as **rougaille**. It is a brittle delicacy with a slightly burnt flavour, made from manioc (cassava root). The last factory, or rather cottage industry, that still makes it dates back to 1870. There are now as many as five flavours: butter, milk, chocolate, coconut and custard. As it is rather dry, some butter or jam helps. Some European tourists find it not sweet enough, and many prefer to eat it with cheese.

Bol déviré/renversé - only available in Chinese restaurants since at home it is pointless to eat food in this fashion. This dish is comprised of rice, meat, Chinese sausages, vegetables and sauce served in a bowl that is turned upside down on a plate.

Boulette poisson/vanyan - fish balls, in soup or cooked with vegetable dishes. On their own, sold by street vendors along with a hot soup and chilli sauce (C).

Brède - this term covers all edible leaves: **brède décine** (Chinese leaves), **brède crésson** (watercress), **sousou** (chow chow), **mouroume** (murung), **ziromon** (pumpkin), **malbar, martin, mamzel**, among others. Depending upon where you eat **brède**, it is either stir-fried or **toufée** (braised *à la mauricienne*).

Bouyon brède - **brède** are also used to make a clear soup which is drunk with food (to wash it down). It may be flavoured with bones, cheap cuts of meat, and increasingly with **ajinomoto** (monosodium glutamate).

Briani - the Mauritian version of this well known spicy rice dish is also made with fish or venison. Big chunks of beef or lamb, cooked slowly in huge pots mixed with potatoes, ginger, onion, cinammon, turmeric. Usually eaten with salad, **zasar** or **satini**. This is a dish for special occasions as it takes so long to cook.

Cacapizon - another example of the crude Mauritian sense of humour. Literally translated it means pigeon's droppings! A fried snack made of gram flour which resembles fresh pigeon's mess (I).

Calamindas - local candy floss, sold by street or bicycle vendors.

Carri - generally any dish, including curry, which is eaten with other staple foods, such as rice, bread, **farata**. **Masala**, the mixture of spices that forms the basis of curry, is the word more often used locally for curry, although since the arrival of tourists curry (still pronounced **carri**) is becoming more popular. This term can confuse a visitor, for a Mauritian who offers to cook a **carri poul** may mean a dish made with chicken rather than a chicken curry. In a restaurant, **carri laviane** (with meat) can be made of beef, lamb, chicken, venison but rarely pork. There may still be restaurants where chicken curry, which all meat-eating islanders eat, is known as **carri No.1**. But beware of **carri No.2** on the menu: it is made with monkey meat! This is a delicacy enjoyed mainly by Creoles.

Since **carri** is eaten daily, it has become part of Creole slang, of which the following are examples:
Pa mo carri - I don't fancy it/him/her
Arranze so carri - to punish somebody
Do not confuse **cari poulé** with chicken curry. This is the name of a plant whose leaves resemble those of the bay tree and are used to season curry and stew.

Colfi malai - a sort of ice cream, a Mauritian version of kulfi, sold by vendors after nightfall (a disappearing trade). The name may be a corrupt rendering of 'cold cream and ice'.

Confi - an example of a French culinary preparation that has been Creolized out of all recognition. In French, *confit* refers to crystallized fruit, conserve of duck and duck's liver, as well as pickled gherkins. In Mauritius it means mainly pickled chillies, half-ripe fruit and vegetables such as cucumbers and carrots. These are preserved in vinegar, with green chillies and salt, and eaten at any time, even as a dessert, with a generous sprinkling of chilli sauce mixed with salt.

Croquette - pieces of meat or vegetable fried in batter and served hot. **Croquette volail** (chicken) is a favourite local finger buffet. This is another French term which has undergone a complete change of meaning. In France you would expect a *croquette* to be made of chocolate. There are also all sorts of fritters, known as **gato** (F. *gâteau*) made of sliced vegetables, fruit, or even sliced bread. Eg **gato brinzel** (aubergine), **gato patate** (sweet potato), **gato banane** (banana). See below.

Dhal puri - without doubt this is the Mauritians' favourite snack. A pancake cooked over a low fire on a **tawa** and stuffed with a purée of split peas. Eaten with a **rougaille** or **satini** (I), on sale everywhere. Do not leave Mauritius without trying it!

Dipain - bread of all kinds. **Dipain maison** - traditional roundish bread roll. **Dipain**

moule - rectangular or tin-shaped, with a crusty top.

Dipain frire - a Creole snack or **gajak**. Slices of bread (normally stale, hence firmer) fried in batter. The dots of greenery are chopped chillies and spring onion. Eaten with a hot **satini** or **rougaille**.

Dité lavani - locally grown tea flavoured with vanilla. Try it at least once. Most tourists find it so refreshing and like it so much they buy the tea to take home. Cynics say the tea used is of inferior quality, which is why it has to be flavoured.

Fangourin - fresh sugar cane juice. Not generally on sale but can be tasted whilst visiting a sugar factory, or ask a friend living near a factory to get you some. Only available during harvest time, July - December. Much better to get a piece of fresh cane and chew the juice out of its fibre.

Farata - the Mauritian version of paratha. Unleavened flat bread with several layers. Made of plain flour and water. Real Indian paratha is richer, containing ghee and spices.

Gajak - snacks: anything from fried **wantan** to **samoussa** (see below).

Gato - cakes of every description, even some confectionery. **Gato francé** is a collective name for locally made European style patisserie. They used to be the most expensive snacks, sold only in *patisseries*, but no longer. The arrival of fast-food outlets such as Kentucky Fried Chicken has somehow downgraded **gato francé**.

Gato coco - squarish, multi-coloured confectionery made of sugar and grated coconut.

Gato costé - another sugary confectionery cut into small cubes.

Gato cravat - fried pastry in the shape of a bow tie. Sweet or savoury (C).

Gato lacire - sweetish ground rice cake resembling wax in colour. Wax for floor polish used to be sold cut into small pieces which looked like this cake. At Chinese New Year, you can try it for free in Chinese shops! It has become a tradition for Chinese shopkeepers to give pieces of it to their customers at this festival.

Gato laline (F. *la lune*) - Chinese moon cakes, eaten during the Chinese mid-autumn festival; now available throughout the year in specialist shops.

Gato manioc - sweet, soft flat cake, made of grated manioc (cassava).

Gato mariaze - a collective name for any cakes eaten at a wedding reception, including the traditional Western tiered wedding cake.

Gato moutail - red or brownish (depending on whether white or brown sugar is used), syrupy cake sold in markets and such places. The pieces are intertwined and piled high. Very sticky! (I)

Gato napolitaine - probably the most famous **gato francé** but cannot be French as you will not find it in France. Nor is it from Naples since Italian tourists are puzzled by its name. It is a kind of round shortbread biscuit, sandwiched with locally made jam **lazlé** (F. *la gelée*) and covered in pink icing. A must.

Gato pimen - another great Mauritian favourite. Contrary to expectation its main ingredient is not chilli but ground split peas. When combined with chopped chillies, onion, spring onion and spices, the effect is a unique and mouth-watering bite-sized savoury *amuse-gueule*. This small, round, flattish fried cake (best eaten piping hot) is a ubiquitous **gajak** found sizzling everywhere. Go for the seller with the longest queue, as there is a big difference in taste and flavour between the best and the mediocre.(I). Warning: this **gajak** is addictive!

Gato zinzam - sticky, dark pieces of ginger cake (C).

Goolabjamoon - small, sausage shaped cake made of milk and flour, and steeped in syrup (I).

Kucha - see **zasar**.

Lasoup - instead of **bouyon brède**, which is easier to prepare, Mauritians may take soup with their meals. A Creole speciality is made with a variety of pulses which are boiled to a stew with bones, or salted or cheap meat to give flavour, and seasoned with thyme, coriander, ginger and fried onion and garlic.

Macachia - sweet bread roll. Some contain grated coconut and raisins, best eaten still warm. Vendors bicycle along the streets laden with them, chanting: **so bouyante macachia so, coco raisin, coco raisin.** (Hot, piping hot **macachia**, coconut and raisin). If you leave your hotel and venture out, you might be lucky enough to encounter this rapidly disappearing breed of salesmen.

Maspain - the Mauritian version of madeira cake, usually with a topping of icing. A **gato francé**.

Minn frire/chow minn - Chinese style fried egg noodles with meat, shrimp and other garnishes. Now sold even by pavement vendors. For genuine Sino-Mauritian **chow minn** go to a Chinese restaurant.

Moulkoo - intertwined, crisp, savoury cake made of gram flour.

Nan - another version of unleavened bread (I).

Oundé/poundé - small, sweet Indian cake sold by street vendors.

Palmis (F. *coeur de palmiste/palmier*) - the main ingredient of salad of kings is the tender shoot of the top half of a 5-year-old palm tree which is killed solely for its 'heart'. Although grown in Mauritius, mainly on sugar estates, restaurants may serve tinned **palmis** probably imported from South America. Only top hotels may have the genuine local article. **Zasar palmis**, imported in tins from Réunion, is a great delicacy, eaten with **dipain maison**.

Pao - Chinese steamed cake/dumpling with a filling of meat (savoury) or bean paste (sweet).

Piao - small round cake, crunchy on the outside, syrupy inside, sold in shops (C).

Pistas griyé - another ubiquitous Mauritian favourite, sold by peanut sellers everywhere. Dry-fried peanuts with pink skin. Delicious! Peanuts are also sold boiled in their shells.

Poujine maille - ground maize cake sold by street vendors. A spongy, moist, sweet yellow cake with raisins and vanilla, cut into triangles, topped with grated coconut.

Poutou - round or bun-shaped ground rice sweet cake, plain or sprinkled with grated coconut. Sold by street vendors, and in shops (I).

Puri - Indian savoury fried pancake eaten with **rougaille**.

Rissole - crescent-shaped fried savoury cake with various fillings, but normally filled with salmon, chopped onion and pepper. Sold in *tabagies*, (**tabazi**) It may also be offered at more upmarket receptions or cocktail parties as a **gajak**.

Roti - Mauritians must eat hundreds of thousands of these thin, savoury pancakes which are sold everywhere. This great favourite is eaten with **rougaille** and other **carri** made of **brède sonze** and pulses. Ask the vendor to remove the small chillies! If you eat these **roti** in the Port Louis market, **(bazar central)**, wash them down with coconut water, on sale at nearby stalls, for a truly Creole gastronomic experience.

Rougaille - this Creole invention has been described by European travel writers as anything cooked with tomatoes *à la provençale*. If it started life as such, **rougaille** has become the most Mauritian of dishes. Even the word seems to be a Creole creation. Its base or main ingredient is the local tomato **pom damour** (love apple), plus just about every local herb - garlic, onion, chilli, thyme, coriander leaves, ginger - which are cooked until all flavours are well diffused. It may be eaten on its own or with any meat, fish, even **gato pimen**. No **dhal puri, roti, farata** or other savoury cakes would be the same without it. It is probably eaten daily by most Mauritians. Some hotels and restaurants have started calling it **lasauce Creole** or **lasauce rouze**.

Salad - most Creole meals are eaten with a salad as a side dish, made up of the various vegetables or fruit that are so plentiful on the island. One great Creole salad is made of octopus. Beware - most salads contain chillies!

Samoussa - usually smaller and crispier than the version sold in Britain. The filling is less rich, usually vegetarian, consisting of pieces of curried potato. A more expensive fish version is available in some places. **Samoussa, dhal puri** and **gato pimen** are the trinity of **gajak** that Mauritians cannot resist - the very sight of them makes them hungry. It is said that if a Mauritian man is offered a choice of these or sex, he will accept both, but will devour the **gajak** first, then relish the woman!

Satini - this is often described as a chutney for want of a better word, but is nothing like the chutneys found in Britain made of apples, green tomatoes and raisins. It is anything but sweet, and the best **satini** is ground on a stone (see **ros carri**). When this is not available, a popular **satini** is made with finely chopped tomatoes mixed with chopped green chillies, onion, coriander leaves and even crushed garlic. Oil is added to bring out the flavour. **Satini** is also made with green fruit, cucumber, carrot, corned beef, tinned tuna or sardine; a delightful **satini** is one made of grilled salted snoek fish. **Satini coco**, however, made of ground fresh coconut and tamarind as the main ingredients, is something of an acquired taste for visitors. A truly Creole dish.

Tamarinade - a local drink made of tamarind pulp and drunk ice cold with a pinch of salt mixed with chilli sauce. Have a sip before committing yourself!

Vindaye - of Portuguese origin (*vinha d'alhos*), it has been adapted and given a Creole name **vin d'ail** (garlic wine). It is pronounced **vinn daille** but is commonly spelt on menus as in the heading. Fried fish (or octopus) is marinated in a mixture of oil, vinegar, garlic, onion, green chillies, crushed mustard seeds and other spices. Can be preserved for weeks, which improves the taste. Not to be confused with vindaloo!

Wantan - minced meat and spices wrapped in thin pastry. Eaten fried as a **gajak** or in hot soup as a *tiffin* or *entrée* (C).

Zasar (F. *achard*) - a Creole vegetarian version of **vindaye.** It is made of vegetables or green fruit or the two combined and marinated in a mixture of oil and spices similar to those of **vindaye**. Served as a side dish. Take care not to drip the sauce which contains saffron on your clothes - the stain can be stubborn! **Kucha** is a variation, usually made with green fruit.

RECENT ADDITIONS TO CREOLE

Mauritius is known as a 'melting pot' and its inhabitants, who came mainly from Europe, Africa, India and China, brought their languages with them. The majority still speak their respective tongues, if only at home. An exception are the Creoles, descendants of black slaves, a number of whom also have European, Chinese or Indian blood. Their 'native' tongue has always been Mauritian Creole.

With two-thirds of the population being of Indian origin, as opposed to only two per cent Franco-Mauritians, who are now outnumbered even by the Chinese, it was inevitable that while Mauritian French has remained relatively unchanged for years, Creole is acquiring more Indian and Chinese words. However, despite the fact that there are only a few hundred English people currently living in Mauritius, more English words are being Creolized than any others. The reason is the use of English in pop songs, American films and IT. This is at a time when the English language itself is being used less and less on the island. See *The History of Mauritius and its Languages*.

Mauritian Creole does not appear to be fussy where it gets its new words from. Whilst the use of certain recent additions can be explained, for example **ajinomoto**, a Japanese trade name, there is no ready explanation for others except that the islanders like the words and have adopted them. For example the Italian word *ciao*, (meaning both hello and cheerio) was widely adopted long before the comparatively recent influx of Italian tourists, from whom the islanders might have picked it up. One can only guess that they must have heard it in a film.

The words included in this section have been incorporated into Creole approximately since World War II and are readily understood by most islanders. Others are words which have entered the lingua franca perhaps in the last decade. They may be Indian words spoken by, say, Indo-Mauritians who themselves do not speak Indian but employ certain words which are regarded as fashionable when speaking Creole to each other. Such words are increasingly being picked up and used by the rest of the population. An example is **dada**, an Indian word meaning grandfather. Where appropriate, an explanatory note will be given.

Where the origin of the word is not obvious, and if known, it will be given and, if necessary, repeated. As explained elsewhere, initials will usually be used, eg C for Chinese, E - English, F - French, I - Indian, M - Muslim. Where Indian is given as the origin of a word, this includes the various dialects spoken on the island such as Marathi, Tamil, Telegu. Muslim is used instead of Indian where this is deemed more appropriate. Where the literal meaning of a Creole word is considered useful, it is given.

This list is not exhaustive but serves to show some words of recent inclusion, or which are currently in the process of being Creolized. Many such new additions will be found throughout the book, in particular in the chapter *A taste of Mauritius*, and may therefore not be repeated here.

Ah souk/souk souk - uncle (C)

Ajinomoto - Japanese trade name for flavour enhancer monosodium glutamate

Atcha - Good, well (I)

Baboo - a respectful term of address for an older man (I)

Babysit - as in English

Baju - traditional Muslim shirt

Baksis/baktis - something free or a little extra, eg an additional tomato thrown in by the vendor (baksheesh - I)

Bas - enough (I)

Beta - boy, son, friend (I)

Beti - girl, daughter (I)

Bhai - 1. a strong man; 2. an influential male; 3. a good friend (I)

Bhojpuri - Indian dialect spoken by a majority of Indo-Mauritians.

Bibi - 1. a common Muslim term for a girl, may form part of her first name; 2. a woman gardener/sweeper

Bismila - in the name of God (M)

Bonis - bonus (E)

Booking - reservation, as in English

Bisness/bisnessman - as in English

Bye - as in English

Cabaille - traditional Chinese dress still worn by older Chinese women not born in Mauritius. Also referred to as **linze pizama**. It consists of a tunic and trousers

Calpa - wooden sandals (I)

Caria - termite (I)

Carom - a kind of miniature snooker board game played by flicking counters with fingers (from the trade mark)

Catcam - a mixture of spices wrapped in betel leaf which some Indians chew

Catora - metal food container, used mainly by Indians to take food to work (I)

Cavadi - decorated bamboo or wooden structure seen during Tamil festivals, which are carried on the shoulders of pilgrims (I)

Cawal - a Muslim party of music and singing. The term is now used for any such party

Chacha - paternal uncle (I). Sir Seewoosagur Ramgoolam, the Father of the Nation, was known affectionately by all as **chacha**

Check/cheké - as in English, to check; also a cheque

Chong sam - a tight-fitting high-necked dress with slits at the sides (C)

Chow minn - Chinese style fried noodles

Ciao - cheerio, see you (Italian)

Computer - as in English

Coustic - somersault (I)

Coyok - Chinese medicine: a brown/black paste used to reduce inflammation

Curidar - traditional Indian dress consisting of a tunic, trousers and a shawl

Cus - trousers worn by Muslim women

Dada - paternal grandfather (I)

Degré - a university qualification, degree (E)

Desbin - dustbin (E)
Dhobi - laundryman (I)
Dhoti - traditional Hindu loin-cloth, still worn by old Indian men in villages, also known as **langouti**
Divali - Hindu festival of light
Dividen - dividend
Fair deal - as in English
Family planning - as in English
Fax - as in English
Filling - a petrol filling station
Flat - apartment (E)
Foung pao - little red envelopes containing money given by Chinese at New Year
Gamat - celebrations with music and traditional food on the eve of Indian and Muslim wedding
Godam - a warehouse (I)
Gol - goal, as in English
Goli - goalkeeper (E)
Godsev - British national anthem
Harftime - half-time (E)
Holi - Hindu festival
Id - Muslim holy days (Eid-ul-Fitr & Eid-ul-Doha)
Iman - Muslim priest
Jalsa - an Indian celebration with food and music; now used for any festivities
Kaisé? - how are you? (I)
Kailasson - Tamil temple
Koko - older brother (C)
Lascar/laskarinne m/f - originally a Muslim trader, now a pejorative word for a Muslim
Maja - exciting (I)
Majid - a mosque
Malbar - originally an Indian from Malabar, now a pejorative term for an Indian
Mamou - maternal uncle (I)
Marathi - a marathi-speaking Indian; the language
Maraz/marazine m/f - an Indian priest of Brahmin caste
Masala - spices used as basis for curry powder (I), a more common word for curry
Naiba - there is none (I), I haven't any
Namasté - salutation, Indian greeting used as hello and goodbye
Namaz - the act of praying by Muslim
Nana - 1. maternal grandmother (I); 2. baby language for eating
Nika - Muslim wedding ceremony
Okay/OK - this English colloquialism, made famous in Mauritius by American films, is probably heard on the island as often as in England
Om - Hindu sacred syllable
One-man show - as in English
One off - as in English

Pagla/pagli m/f - loony (I)
Paisa - money (I)
Pak - betel nut (I)
Pandit - Hindu priest
Pani - water, rain (I)
Panjabi - traditional Muslim women's dress; the language
Papadam - pappadom, Indian crisp pancake
Penalty - as in English
Pinpong - table tennis, from the trade mark
Pongal - Tamil New Year
Puja - Hindu prayer
Rajput - considered a low cast Indian in Mauritius
Ramadan - Muslim month of fasting
Red tape - as in English
Saheb - Sir, Lord (I)
Salam - Arabic salutation, see you, cheerio
Sali - concrete floor (I)
Samoussa - samosa
Sapsoowhy/sapsiwhy - Chinese shuttlecock played with the foot
Sardar - overseer, especially of field workers (I)
Sari - a Hindu woman's chief garment
Satini - chutney (E) but the Mauritian version is quite a different dish. See *A taste of Mauritius*
Scanner - as in English
Sir - as in English
Sit - monthly savings club among friends/colleagues/club members who meet each month and take turns to have the money collected each month (I)
Sit-in - as in English
Sivaratri - Hindu festival
Sit fan - eat a meal/food, meal time (literally: eat rice) (C)
Squatter - as in English
Swami - Hindu priest
Tabla - small drum
Tambi - younger brother (I)
Tawa - flat circular metal implement for cooking **farata, dhal puri** (I)
Tchoy - 1. any Chinese leaf vegetable; 2. a dish to accompany rice
Team - as in English
Tika - a red mark seen on forehead of married Hindu women, now used more and more as a beauty spot. Also known as **potu**
Titi - older sister (C)
Tookmaria - gelatinous seeds used in **alouda** (I). See *A taste of Mauritius*
Topless - as in English
Ugadi - Telegu New Year
User-friendly - as in English
Warning - as in English

CHILDREN'S CREOLE

Baba - baby
Cadak/cadadac - piggy back
Caicoune - dead
Canette - marbles
Casiette - to hide
Cap lécol - to play truant. **Ene capaire lécol** is a child who frequently plays truant
Caspat - on all fours, on hands and knees (F. *quatre pattes*)
Cause menti - to lie
Colcamani - children's transfer (F. *décalcomanie*)
Coqsis/cotok - tapping a child's head with the back of a folded index finger
Cram cram - crunchy
Dodo - sleep
Fass/fassé - we're no longer friends (F. *faché*)
Gorer - to cheat in class by copying another's work
Guélar - a cry-baby, a bigger child who still cries
Guyling guyling - a rattling toy
Lamé gaté - a child who cannot leave things alone
Lou lou - wolf
Lougarou - werewolf
Louké - to peep
Nana - food; (*verb*) to eat
Pipi - urine; (*verb*) to urinate
Saute mouton - leap frog
Tata - faeces, excrement
Ti bonomme - little boy
Tou tou - little dog
Zouer couq/couq casiette - to play hide and seek (F. *coucou, cache-cache*)

CREOLE CREOLE

After you have got used to the sound of Mauritian Creole, it will not take long before you will notice that some people repeat a word twice. This is yet another peculiarity of the language, as if certain words require this emphasis to get their full meaning across.

Readers will find this 'double Creole speak' in the pages of this book. A few examples are given below in order to acquaint you with the more common ones that you are likely to hear in conversation with Mauritians. Where it is felt necessary, examples of how they are used are given.

Caré caré (F. *carrément*) - to the point, frank. **Dire moi caré caré** - tell me without beating about the bush

Cata cata/cata catac - 1. a grasshopper; 2. to create a fuss. **Bon, pa bizin faire cata catac are sa** - alright, there's no need to make a fuss over it

Catia catia/catia catiac - a percussion instrument used in sega

Caya caya - 1. to shuffle; 2. creased, either a wrinkled face or crumpled clothing. **Li finn alle danser avec ene sémize caya caya** - he has gone to the dance wearing a crumpled shirt

Couyon couyon - not very bright. **Li impé couyon couyon sa mem dimoune coquin li tou létan** - he's a bit stupid that's why people are always cheating him

Craze crazé/cass cassé - looking shabby/old. **Mo papa en bonne santé malgré so laze, mé linn impé craze crazé** - my father's in good health despite his age but he's looking a bit old

Enba enba - an exclamation heard during sega dancing. The male partner shouts "enba enba!" to invite his partner to crouch down to her knees with him

Faille faille - a little ill. **Li parraite impé faille faille zordi** - she looks a little unwell today

Fan faner - to circulate, scatter, disperse. **La police vini la, fan faner** - the police are coming, let's disperse

Fem fem - an effeminate man, a little effeminate

Fou fou - a little mad. If **fou** is not repeated, then the person is really mad! **Pa pren li conte, li fou fou sa** - don't take any notice of him, he's a bit loony

Gidi gidi/ gidi gidic - to tickle. **So lizié faire moi gidi gidi** - her eyes tickle my fancy

Goonoo goonoo - tadpole

Guyling guyling - musical triangle, toy

Lou lou - wolf

Mal mal - if the worst comes to the worst

Malade malade - literally ill ill. What this is meant to convey depends on the tone of the speaker and where s/he places the emphasis. Said quickly, it means not too well, so so, not his own self. Where the second **malade** is emphasized, it means the person is suffering from more than a simple illness. This is often used in the negative. Eg in describing the sudden death of a person, the speaker may say that the deceased was not really that seriously ill - **li pa ti malade *malade*.**

Marce marcer - stroll. **Li finn alle marce marcer dan parc** - he has gone for a stroll in the park.

Souk souk - baby's dummy

Tam tam - musical drum

Tec tec - small bivalve shells. **Lasoup tec tec** - soup made with these shells.

Tou tou - a young dog

Triste triste - a little sad. **Li impé triste triste dépi qui so mari finn allé** - she's a bit sad since her husband left.

Vacarne vacarner(F. *vacancier*?) - going out with friends. **Mo frère finn alle vacarne vacarner dan boi** - my brother has gone out with his friends to the wood.

Zozo - stupid

ARCHAIC FRENCH

This chapter provides some examples of French that baffle even the French. Whilst the French spoken in France has been evolving all the time, that spoken in Mauritius has evolved differently and perhaps more slowly. This is not surprising as it has always been the language of a minority. On the other hand, the more dominant Creole continues to evolve to this day.

Thus many French words have retained the meanings they had in the early 18th century, at the time of the first French settlers. It is also a fact that many of the French words still in use today were originally naval terms, such as *hisser* and *larguer*. Paradoxically, whilst some of these early French words have retained their original sound and spelling, they have at the same time acquired another, more modern meaning. As if designed to confuse non-Mauritians, many such words have also kept their true French meaning and both may be used by the islanders.

For example, in modern French *guetter* means to watch carefully or to watch (out) for, but in Mauritius it is more commonly used in the sense of to see, to look: **Guetter, madame, zoli zoli flaire par ici** - look, madam, lovely flowers here; **Guetter si mo énan laclé lacaze dan mo caba** - see if I've got the house key in my handbag.

Mauritian French	English	Modern French
anneau (**zano**)	earring	boucle d'oreille
auto	car	voiture (more common)
camper	not necessarily spending the night in a tent but includes spending a few days in a house by the sea, known as a **campement**	camping
casser	to pick/gather fruit/flower	cueillir
causer	to talk, speak	parler
dégager	to hurry up	dépêcher
galoper	to run	courir
guetter	to look, see	regarder
hisser	to pull	tirer
guerre	argument, scuffle	querelle
larguer	to undo, let go	lâcher
mari	husband as well as the superlative for anything out of the ordinary	mari
parer	ready	prêt
percer	to wring out	presser
pied	a plant of any size, tree	pied, arbre
roder	to search, look for	chercher
soulier	shoe	chaussure (more common)
tailler	to cut	couper

TRUNCATED FRENCH

There are many French words in use in Mauritius which have been shortened and may not therefore be readily recognisable even by the French. Some are so different that even Mauritians do not realise how these words came about. The reason for their being 'truncated' is probably due to their being 'too long' in the first place and the original slaves found them too difficult to remember and/or to pronounce. Although this is but a guess, it makes sense as speakers of any language tend to shorten some words, eg phone for telephone, deli for delicatessen and so on.

After all a shorter word in a strange language is definitely easier to say. This is another example of Mauritian Creole 'eating' French words and why the French find that Mauritians speak too fast.

Below are just a few examples. As you learn more Creole and listen to people speaking it, you will notice more. If you already know French, make a point of looking out for them.

Creole	Original French	English
asté	acheter	to buy
banané	bonne année	Happy New Year
bis	autobus	bus
bitasion	habitation	This originally referred to dwellings on sugar plantations. It has since become a synonym for villages, small towns. **Li sorte bitasion sa** - he/she is from a village, has the connotation that people from the country are not as bright as those from bigger towns
blier	oublier	to forget
ladan	là dedans	inside
parer	préparer	to prepare
tarder	retarder	to delay
tasser	attacher	to tie up, fasten
traper	attraper	to hold, catch

NOT IN FRONT OF THE LADIES (OR CHILDREN)!

Mauritians like swearing. They utter profanities all the time and Creole swearwords are quite descriptive and succinct. Most of the curses refer to the genitalia of the person swearing or to those of the mother or sister of the person being sworn at. For some strange reason, the islanders seem to delight in teaching foreigners their worst swearwords and then watch in glee as they repeat them innocently where they should not, such as in front of ladies, or worse, to them!

Many offensive-sounding profanities, however, are not meant to insult; they just form part of some people's vocabulary; the user hopes they will be interpreted as a sign of his virility. It is quite normal for conversation, especially among young men, to contain vulgarities. In Mauritius you will hear people greeting their friends with an expletive, eg, **Et ta couyon, cote to pé aller?** (Hey, you fool, where are you off to?). People becoming impatient in a restaurant for the waiter to bring their orders may be heard complaining: **Cote sa bèze so mama garson la?** (Where is this fuck-his-mother waiter?) The waiter is unlikely to take offence if he overhears this.

If you do not want to get caught out - read this section. It includes several words you are likely to hear (hopefully not addressed to you!), as well as other words that may better be termed 'naughty'. They are not quite expletives but they are usually sex-related, and are best not repeated in front of women or children, or indeed people you have only just met.

Some expressions which sound particularly rude or outrageous may have been 'devalued' because they have become so common, and are even used by children who may not realise their full meaning. Mauritians employ curses to make their idiom more colourful and they are not necessarily meant to hurt or offend. The islanders also tend to swear as much at inanimate objects as at people or animals. Someone who has been waiting for a long time for a bus may be heard cursing: **Cote sa liki so mama bis la été?** (Where's that cunt of its mother's bus?). Remember, some vulgar words are only offensive if said to the wrong people, that is women and children.

Should a foreigner try to be as foul-mouthed as the locals? Only if you are sure of the correct 'strength' of the terms of abuse that you intend to use. This can only come from practice and from mixing with Mauritians of your own status, age and sex. The best advice is to play safe and smile, even if you feel you are being sworn at. You can always swear back in your own language, which the locals may not understand.

In an attempt to help the student of Mauritian Creole, a system of grading is employed to denote how strong a swearword is, using a scale of 1 to 4, as follows:
1.   Can be used to impress
2.   Quite forceful - use with care
3.   Strictly amongst the lads; not in front of ladies or children
4.   Best avoided! .
Only terms of abuse which require a grading have one of these numbers allocated to them.

First some Creole words frequently used in vulgarities are given; these are usually anatomical or associated with sex.

Arse/posterior - **tonkin, fes, quinquin**
Breasts - **tété, doudou, manzer ti baba** (lit. baby's food)
Brothel - **loca**
Buttocks (of a woman) - **bofor** (E. buffer)
Clitoris - **bisik** (Creole?)
Circumcision - **catna** (I)
Condom - **capot**
Copulate/have sexual intercourse - **capsail, coco, cacabol, faire malice** (do not confuse with **foupa malice**, a person with a couldn't-care-less attitude)
Erection - **raid**
Female genitals - **soosout, falou, liki** (F. *le cul*), **catail, languette, zouézoué, tootun, poondé** (I)
Loose woman - **gran dilo**
Masturbate, to - **brénner, cass col** (In old French: *se faire malice tout seul* = to masturbate; in Mauritian Creole **malice** is the equivalent of to copulate)
Menstrual periods - **laline** (F *la lune*)
Mistress - **fam gardé**
Over-sexed - **pitasié**
Penis - **gogot, coq, coonouk, bibit, barbara, banane, zozo, laqué, cabo, lazoze, tonton zoze, toulouk, zoué zoué, la mance vente** (lit. belly's handle)
Prostitute - **pitain, niméro**
Sexual pleasure - **gagne bon**
Testicles - **grenne, plok**

Avoye (F. *envoyer*) **moi faire foute** (1) - get lost, leave me alone
Bez (1) - damn. **Mo dan gran bez** - I'm in big trouble. Also means copulate when used with the name of a person, as in next item
Bez so mama (2) - damn his mother; fuck his mother. Usually said in the absence of the person it is meant for
Bézé (1) - to express disappointment, to be in financial trouble. **Ala bézé la, mo finn bliér mo portfeil lacase** - damn, I've left my wallet at home
Bour to mama/to saire (4) - fuck your mother/sister
Bourli (3) - fuck him/her
Bous to fes (2) - shut your arse
Brénnerre (2) - a masturbator, only good at playing with himself
Caca fes (2) - a useless person
Cass so fes (2) - smash his arse
Céqui to liki conten (3) - whatever pleases your pussy
Couyonnade (1) - rubbish, not worth it
Couyonnaire (1) - a scoundrel, dishonest person
Craze so disef (2) - to give somebody a violent beating (lit. smash his balls)
Ene zoli paire manzer ti baba (1) - a nice pair of boobs

Falou (Malagasy) **to mama** (3) - your mother's cunt
Fam (1) - 1. a female who is no longer a virgin; 2. an effeminate man; 3. a weakling/ coward (see **femfem** elsewhere)
Fes cassé (2) - smashed arse, a despicable man
Fézer (1) - a show-off, an arrogant man
Fifi - a gay man, effeminate. Also **tifi tifi**. (F. *fille*)
Flaire - vulgarity (lit. flower). **Sac foi qui li ouver so la bous, flaire qui sorti** - every time he opens his mouth, vulgarity comes out
Fou pa mal (1) - don't give a damn
Grénnaire (2) - an unreliable, useless person (lit. a testicle breaker)
Gro gogot (2) - big penis. **Ti gogot** (F) - small penis
Latète to papa (1) - your father's head, mild swearing term, usually to express disbelief. Equivalent to 'pigs can fly'
Liki to mama/languette to mama (3) - your mother's cunt
Li larze sa (3) - said of a woman who has been penetrated by many men; her vagina has been enlarged. Also used to refer to a goal keeper who lets in a lot of goals. (lit. s/he is wide [open])
Macro (1) - a pimp; one who spills secrets
Mo bour to mama/to saire (4) - I fuck your mother/sister
Mo caca lorli/toi (3) - I shit on him/you
Mo cass to fes (3) - I'll smash your arse
Mo pisser/mo pisser are toi (3) - I don't give a shit (lit. I piss on you)
Niméro sis (1) - No.6, a male homosexual
Pilon (1) - a male homosexual
Pitain (1) - a whore
Sa ene languette so mama sa (2) - he's a cunt of his mother
Soosout pomé (2) - well-rounded female genitals, as revealed by a woman wearing tight-fitting bikini
Souce mo grenne/gogot (4) - suck my balls/prick
Soucerre fes (3) - arse licker, a toady, sycophant
To mama so liki pé grater la? (4) - Is your mother's cunt itching?
Trape mo grenne/gogot (4) - squeeze my balls/prick. This is usually said while the speaker demonstrates by cupping his own genitals
Traverre - bent, a homosexual man

THE HISTORY OF MAURITIUS
AND ITS LANGUAGES

This is only a brief history of Mauritius, included here to give readers a better understanding of Mauritian Creole. It is written essentially from the perspective of the island's people and their languages. It begins with the arrival of the first settlers on the island and ends with the present time, with movements afoot in Mauritius to formalize Creole into an official, written language. The Bibliography at the end contains several history books for anyone who wishes to read further onto the subject.

Mauritius is a volcanic island which, from 1,000 AD, was known to Arab sailors trading from Zanzibar. Even as the country celebrated the 400th anniversary of the Dutch first landing there on 20 September 1598 and naming it Mauritius, the Omanis were claiming that it was they, not the Dutch, who were the first to occupy the island. The Arabs assert that they have documents to prove that by the 15th century their kingdom in the Indian Ocean included Madagascar, the Comoros and Mauritius. There is no dispute that the Arab merchants, who sailed the ocean in their dhows, had the earliest records of the existence of the island. Their early charts list it under at least three different names: Dina Robin, Dina Margabin and Dina Arobi.

The Portuguese started to chart the Indian Ocean from the early 16th century and many islands in the region still bear the names given then. They are known collectively as the Mascarenhas islands, after Captain Peco Mascarenhas. In 1507 Fernandez Pereira found Mauritius uninhabited and named it *Ilha do Cerne* (Isle of the Swan) after the name of his ship, (and not after the dodo as some history books state). But the only reminder left of the Portuguese presence in Mauritius is to do with this big, flightless bird which they found in abundance on the island. They called it *doudo* (simpleton) because, as there were no predators on the island, the bird did not run away when approached by man. While the bird did not survive, the name has, and today the dodo is a universal symbol of extinction. Two other words of Portuguese origin are still very much in use in Mauritian gastronomy: **camaron** (a fresh water crustracean) and **vindaye** (*vinha d'alhos* - see elsewhere) but it is not clear how exactly they entered the language.

THE DUTCH SETTLEMENT

Having claimed the island in 1598, it was not until 1638, 40 years later, that the Dutch East India Company decided to send settlers to Mauritius as a base from which to protect their trading rights and to prevent the English and the French from making further use of it as a port of call.

There were good supplies of fresh water and fruit on the island and the forests provided plentiful timber, particularly ebony. The Dutch brought in slaves from Madagascar to clear the forests and cultivate the land. Such great quantities of Mauritian ebony were sent to Holland that the price dropped sharply and felling had to be curtailed. The Dutch settlement, however, was not a successful one and they left the island in 1658.

In 1664 the Dutch returned to Mauritius and stayed until 1710. They introduced sugar cane, deer, pigs, and monkeys from Java. Sugar was later to become the sole commercial crop of Mauritius and the mainstay of its economy. When the Dutch finally abandoned the island they did not destroy or take everything with them. Many of their domestic animals had escaped and become wild. But by then the Dutch had killed and eaten the dodo into extinction. Other inhabitants who must have been glad to see the Dutch go were the numerous run-away slaves, whom the French settlers were later to call *marrons*. This word is still in use in Creole to mean a fugitive or a worker who absents himself from work.

There is no record to show whether the *marrons* had a smattering of Dutch or spoke a broken form of the language. If they did later mix with the slaves brought by the French, any Dutch they had must have got absorbed into Creole beyond recognition. Today, apart from place names such as Flacq, Plaines Wilhems and Flic-en-Flac, there are hardly any Dutch words in Creole.

THE FRENCH SETTLEMENT 1715-1810

By 1674, the island of Bourbon, a day's sail from Mauritius, had become the *Compagnie des Indes'* main base in the Indian Ocean. In 1715 the French took possession of the unoccupied Mauritius and changed its name to Isle de France. On the site of the old Dutch capital, Noord Wester Haven, they built Port Louis, which still bears the name.

Of the many French governors sent to govern the island, Bertrand Mahé de Labourdonnais was the most capable and successful, and the most popular. His statue has pride of place in the harbour esplanade in Port Louis and many places, such as Mahébourg, have been named after him.

By 1788 the population of Isle de France comprised 7,000 French or white Europeans and 36,000 slaves. The slaves came from Madagascar, Mozambique and other parts of Africa. Some were brought in from as far away as Senegal, on the western coast. Many of the slaves from Africa spoke their Bantu languages and the Creole language contains many words from Bantu, the most famous of which being **sega** (see *Whither Creole?* below). Muslim seamen, known as Lascar, called on the island regularly during the French occupation and some stayed. Mauritian Creole still has the word **lascar** as a pejorative term for Muslim.

As these slaves as well as the Muslims had their own distinct languages and cultures, there must have been a language problem when it came to communicating with each other and with the French. As no one language could get hegemony, a broken French was used out of necessity and this eventually evolved into Creole. The children of the slaves and early immigrant workers would have been the first speakers whose mother tongue was Creole. The first written record of this Creole appeared in a letter written by Baron de Vaux Grant in 1749. According to Bernardin de Saint Pierre in his book *Voyage à l'Isle de France*, by the time he arrived there in 1769, the French patois was already widespread. This is some 50 years after the French brought the first slaves to the island.

Today the Franco-Mauritians, the descendants of the French settlers, are the only ethnic group which can truly claim to be still speaking their mother tongue at home.

This is not surprising considering that French has now been spoken there for 280 years. However, Creole is slowly penetrating even the French households and Creole words are increasingly used in conversation at home 'to add flavour'.

THE BRITISH RULE 1810-1968

In 1809 the British occupied Rodrigues, 350 miles east of Isle de France, which they used as a base the following year to capture Réunion (Bourbon until 1793). It was from the latter that a British force under General Abercrombie set off to capture Isle de France from the French and rename it Mauritius.

If despite a century and a half of British rule Mauritius remains in most aspects more French than English, this is due to the generous capitulation terms offered to the French. They were allowed to keep their property, land, language, law, religion, customs, culture - in fact their way of life was hardly affected.

However, the British insisted that the affairs of government would henceforth be in English. So it could not have been an easy co-habitation to begin with between the vanquished French and the victorious Albions as far as language was concerned. The French were not exactly over-enthusiastic about learning English. This language battle is still going on to this day and English remains a foreign language in Mauritius while the French cultural influence has remained dominant in the island.

Full abolition of slavery in Mauritius did not happen until 1835, when the slave owners, mostly French, received handsome compensation from the British. As the last thing the freed slaves wanted to do was to continue working in the sugarcane fields, the plantation owners quickly had to replace them with indentured labourers. These people were soon arriving from India in such great numbers that before too long they had outnumbered the freed slaves. For some years there was more Indian spoken in a variety of dialects and languages on the island than French and Creole put together. The necessity to communicate with their French employers made it imperative for the Indians to learn to speak the broken French widely used on the island.

POST INDEPENDENCE

Mauritius became a fully independent country on 12 March 1968 but remained a constitutional monarchy headed by the Queen of England. On 12 March 1992, the then Prime Minister Sir Anerood Jugnauth turned the country into a Republic with a Mauritian, Sir Veerasamy Ringadoo, as President and Head of State. In the general election of 1995, which was won by an alliance made up of the *Parti Travailliste* (Labour) and the *Mouvement Militant Mauricien* (MMM), Dr Navin Ramgoolam, Leader of the Labour Partry, became Prime Minister and Paul Bérenger, leader of the MMM, his deputy and Minister of Foreign Affairs. The coalition lasted only 18 months. Bérenger became the Leader of the Opposition while PM Ramgoolam continued to govern.

According to the July 1996 census, the 1,133,721 population of Mauritius was made up of over 50% Hindus, some 35% Creoles, about 16% Muslims, under 3% Chinese and less than 2% French. Creoles are people of mixed race, predominantly descendants of black slaves. Officially they are known as the *population générale*, that is all those who are not of Indian or Chinese descent. This includes a minority group known locally as mulattos, offspring of negroes and Europeans, who have paler complexions, and some of whom may be offended to be referred to as Creole or **milat** (F. *mulâtre*). The politically correct term used to be **métis** but now it would appear that *gens de couleur* (coloured people) is gaining popularity.

Gran blan is sometimes taken, even by Mauritians, to mean people of pure French stock. In fact it refers to Franco-Mauritians who belong to one of the big French families who are immensely wealthy. By implication, **ti blan** means Franco-Mauritians who are not wealthy, though this term is rarely heard.

Irrespective of race, the language that all school children speak is Creole. At primary schools, during the first year at least, instruction is given in Creole. French is introduced gradually, followed by some English, using French and English textbooks. By the time school children sit the all-important Certificate of Primary Education (CPE) exams, which they must pass to go on to secondary school at the age of 11, they are already being taught French and English side by side.

In secondary education, most textbooks are in English, especially in subjects such as science and mathematics which in theory should be taught in English. However, at this level it is not unusual for even English literature to be explained in French by some teachers. By the time children can read, they are brought up on a diet of popular French comics, French films and mostly French-language newspapers. They do not really begin to read English seriously until towards the end of their secondary education.

Chinese and Indian parents who, up to World War II, used to insist that their children must have a Chinese or Indian education, then began to realize that the route to advancemenet at work was through knowing French and English. Not only were Oriental and Asiatic languages not much use in getting a good, well-paid job, but they did not equip the children even to read the newspapers. By Independence, only one of several Chinese schools which existed in the 1950s had survived for those few diehards who were determined that their offspring should have a Chinese education. The rest had transferred their children to the mainstream system of education to give them an equal chance, though many continued to study Chinese at evening classes or by private tuition. Whilst accepting that minority languages are of limited use in the commercial world, parents still tried to ensure that their children did not abandon their ancestors' language and culture. It is thanks to this attitude that so many languages are still spoken on this small island. In fact the issue of 'Oriental' languages took on great political importance in the months leading to the 1995 general election, and today they form part of the CPE exam.

Which language Mauritians speak when they enter the workforce depends on the job. Messengers, cleaners, domestics, drivers, manual workers and so on are likely to use Creole. On the factory floor it is Creole, though supervisors and managers may use French in the office. More often than not telephonists answer in French. In foreign-owned companies (except French ones) the language of the managers is more likely to be English, also used for memos, reports, notices etc simply because the owners are English-speaking.

Most official correspondence, especially with the Civil Service, is still predominantly in English, although the use of French is definitely on the increase. Staff in banks, insurance companies and other conglomerates, especially at managerial level, tend to speak to each other and to answer the phone in French. Bank staff are expected to speak to the public in French unless they are not 'properly dressed', that is not wearing a suit and tie. Men who do tend to receive better treatment everywhere, from shopkeepers, post office clerks, traffic police and so on, and would normally be addressed in French. The same applies to women who are smartly dressed. What one wears can determine in which language one will be greeted in Mauritius!

Politicians are the people most likely to have to use all three languages: Creole, French and English. Their ability to speak the last two, however, may vary considerably. The gift of the gab does not necessarily extend to proficiency in languages other than Creole. English remains the predominant language in the National Assembly, followed by French and, more recently, retorts in Creole have enlivened the House and seem to be becoming more commonplace, probably to the desperation of the stenographer who has to take everything down verbatim.

The following report, of the conclusion of a heated ministerial debate, shows how politicians are now using a mix of languages to achieve maximum effect:

Speaker: Put your question ou je vais sonner la cloche. . .
Bérenger: The Honourable Member is better in tire tapairre lor difil électric.
Duval: Je demande au ministre de retirer ses propos.
Bérenger: To amène tapairre dan rénion.
Duval: Je demande au ministre de retirer ses propos. He is lying.
Speaker: Withdraw the word 'lying'. It's unparliamentary.
Duval: Je retire mes propos. Meet me outside.

In Mauritius people are forgiven for speaking poor English but not for bad French. Hence many politicians, like the former Prime Minister Sir Anerood Jugnauth, stick to English in their formal speeches. When people read politicians' speeches in French in the newspapers, they have been carefully corrected by the journalist. The current Prime Minister, Dr Navin Ramgoolam, who spent many years working in England is fluent and confident in English. One can usually tell where a politician was educated, and those who prefer to make speeches in French are of the new breed of graduates of French universities.

Local radio and TV programmes are mainly in French with repeats of the main news bulletins in English. In addition there are programmes in minority languages. Creole and Bhojpuri, although majority languages, were deemed unsuitable for a long time but are now commonly heard on air; they are ideal for these media as both are spoken languages which are widely understood. Non-Indian films are dubbed in French and a great percentage of Mauritians watch French TV, which they can pick up from Réunion.

French popular songs, Mauritian favourites for a long time, have been overtaken by Anglo-American ones. Indian hits, most of them from films, are of course mostly of interest to Indians, but do not be surprised to find non-Indians whistling the latest popular Indian tunes. Sega music and folk-dance, the only truly Creole culture, is sung in Creole and is now beloved of all Mauritian-born islanders. Some segas are now sung in Bhojpuri, though aficionados dismiss these as akin to Country and Western being sung in Mandarin - "not sega"! Mauritians in France and England have written and translated sega in both languages, but these songs have not caught on. Good sega lyrics contain double meanings and sexual overtones, which are lost in translation. In sega Mauritians have something that only they can fully appreciate: innocent-sounding lyrics with meanings that foreigners do not pick up.

The extent to which the country can be said to be bilingual in French-English can best be seen in semi-formal events such as Rotary meetings. The language in which a meeting is conducted depends on the president's preference, or is dictated by the presence of visitors. Similiarly, a guest speaker is normally free to use either language. The Rotarians themselves converse mostly in French as informal conversation is rarely in English.

In his book *Kreol* (1972) Philip Baker said that his research had shown that the number of mother tongues (that is, the languages spoken by their ancestors on arrival in Mauritius) spoken by the islanders came to 18. They were: Bengali, Bhojpuri, Cantonese, Creole, English, French, Gujerati, Hakka, Hindi, Hindustani, Kokni, Kutchi, Mandarin, Marathi, Punjabi, Tamil, Telegu and Urdu. The 1983 census revealed that the languages spoken daily were: Creole by 521,950; Bhojpuri 197,050 and French 36,048. More recently the official number of languages spoken in Mauritius was given as 19. The country now has a large number of expatriates. However, only a handful of these are spoken daily as a first language in the home from childhood: Creole, Bhojpuri, Chinese, French, Tamil, Marathi and Telegu. The remainder can be grouped as second languages, that is ones acquired later in life. English falls into this category for many Mauritians.

As a result of this rich linguistic heritage, Mauritians whose first language is an Oriental one (in Mauritius this includes Chinese, Indian and their dialects) can usually speak four languages to some extent: Creole, Bhojpuri, French and English. Most others who have completed secondary education will have a working knowledge of English and French in addition to Creole. It is interesting to note that neighbouring countries such as Réunion and Madagascar are not similarly multi-lingual; and visitors to Mauritius often remark how lucky the inhabitants are to be fluent in two of the world's principal languages, French and English.

Tourists are constantly amazed at the extraordinary level of racial tolerance on the island. To a great extent this must be due to the country's common language, Creole, which unites all the races. Of course there are other unifying factors, for example the fact that Mauritians respect and even observe one another's cultures and religions while enjoying complete freedom to practise their own and adore the food of all communities. Hearing people talking another language does not raise eyebrows, so the islanders would not have been surprised to find travel writers describing Mauritius as "a UN in miniature".

However there is a disadvantage in speaking so many languages which is that most Mauritians, with the probable exception of the Frenco-Mauritians, cannot speak any perfectly, or rather correctly. The one language that they are allowed to speak imperfectly is of course Creole, because it is a vernacular without any rules where almost anything is acceptable.

It is gratifying to note that at long last editors of Mauritian newspapers have taken heed of what critics have been telling them to do and are including more English. In the last couple of years journalists have not bothered to translate the whole of their reports, of a court case or of a National Assembly debate, into French for the benefit of their readers. This may be deliberate policy, or it may be due to pressure of time.

One would like to believe that editors are confident their readers know enough English not to skip these 'foreign language' passages, but in any event the English is now quoted verbatim. Quite often the English is neither italicized nor set in quotation marks, as follows:

"Les institutions religieuses sont déjà subventionnées d'un one-off grant d'un million ..."
"Son départ était long overdue."
"Pillay a été cut down to size."
"25% des squatters étaient des genuine cases."
"Il existe encore des Mauriciens qui ne sont pas des law abiding citizens."
"Ces livres ne sont pas user friendly."
"Il y a trop de red tape à Maurice."

Some passages can baffle the reader, who may well wonder which language the journalist is using:

"Suite de la signature d'un traité de non-double imposition avec . . ."

INDIAN LANGUAGES

As mentioned earlier, the first Indians to settle in Mauritius were Muslim seamen during the French occupation. Soon after the British took over, they brought in Indian convicts from other parts of the Empire, such as Penang and Singapore.

It was not until after slavery was abolished in Mauritius, in 1835, that Indian labourers were regularly brought in. They came from all over India, through the ports of Bombay, Madras, Bengal and Calcutta but the exact origins of the first incomers were not recorded. In the second half of the 19th century, many traders, mostly Gujerati Muslims, arrived from Western India.

Hence another Indian dialect arrived with each wave of immigrants, who spoke neither of the island's main languages, French and English. Because of the diversity of dialects, many Indians could not understand each other either, so they had to learn Creole which was far easier to speak than French. It was then that Indian words began to infiltrate Mauritian Creole, such as **gouni** (sack) and **dekti** (cooking pot).

By 1871 Indians made up two-thirds of the population, 216,000 against some 100,000 Africans. Sheer weight of numbers meant that the most widely spoken languages on the island in the last quarter of the 19th century were Indian. But it was not one common language, but included: Bengali, Punjabi, Tamil, Hindi, Telegu and other dialects. Eventually Bhojpuri, a Bengali patois originating in the state of Bihar became dominant. Today Bhojpuri is still spoken by a majority of Indians, including those who have retained their mother tongues as well, such as the Tamils, Marathi and Telegu. In Mauritius Bhojpuri has become the equivalent of what Creole is to French except that, unlike Creole, its use is fast diminishing as the older Indians who speak it die out.

Thus Creole became a hybrid idiom comprehensible to more and more islanders, a living language which did not belong to any ethnic group. Today Indians in Port

Louis and other towns in the Plaines Wilhems district speak more Creole than those in villages and sugar estates, where the majority of Indian field workers and labourers still use Bhojpuri. Nevertheless, nowadays, as Indian children grow up they are tending to speak Creole more.

This shows that travel writers who, after a few days on the island, write that two-thirds of Mauritians speak Indian are not quite right. One can understand and sympathise with outsiders over this misconception when the terms Hindi, Hindu and Hindustani tend to be used loosely and Mauritian Indians refer to themselves as Hindu. It would be more accurate to say that the majority of them can speak the Bhojpuri dialect and a few also speak Hindi and/or other Indian dialects. Hindi is the most common because Indian films, which are avidly watched, are in that language. Also they tend to be more familiar with the vernacular Hindi of films, television and radio than the literary Devanagri Hindi used in Indian books and magazines. The use of Hindi is on the rise as the next generation is being taught it in school. Also increasing numbers of students are going to India for tertiary education, many of whom return with Hindi-speaking wives and children. Some of these Indian-educated Mauritians apparently regard Bhojpuri with disdain, just as educated Creoles used to regard the use of Creole as beneath them.

Gujerati, spoken by a small number of Muslims, is declining. Nor are you likely to hear Urdu on the streets. It is studied by some in the Arabic script, but its use is now restricted mainly to Islamic ceremonies. After the split at Independence of India and Pakistan the Mauritian Indian population likewise re-grouped into Hindu and Muslim communities but this did not have any language consequences; there was no increase in the use of Urdu.

The Mauritian Creole expert Dr Philip Baker noticed that, when speaking Creole Bhojpuri-speakers have a slight phonetic difference not detectable by most listeners. But they also have a habit of using only one form of a verb in Creole. Where there is a short and a long form, for instance **goutte/goutter, alle/aller, manze/manzer**, they tend to use the longer form. It is not incorrect to use either form; it is purely a matter of preference, as can be seen in the numerous examples given elsewhere.

The great drawback to learning Indian, or Chinese for that matter, must be the script and characters. Whilst Indo- and Sino Mauritians may speak their respective tongues, it is easier for them to learn to write a foreign language such as German or Italian. Even if they do master an Oriental language, there are few opportunities to use them and good reading materials are not so readily available.

Nevertheless, some Mauritians have become proficient enough to publish literary works in Hindi, such as Basdeo Bissoondoyal, Bhagat Madhuker, Somdath Buckhory whilst others have become famous outside Mauritius. Abhimanyu Unduth, for instance, the author of some 60 works, is better known overseas as few Mauritians read Hindi for pleasure. Unduth has been showered with decorations and prizes for his poetry, which is studied in several universities. His reputation stretches from India to Trinidad.

CHINESE LANGUAGES
Although the Chinese were amongst the last ethnic groups to settle in Mauritius, they have been present on the island since 1829 when 400 were brought in by the British.

Unlike the Indians, theirs was not a successful settlement and by 1850 only 26 of the original 400 were still on the island.

More Chinese were brought in from the 1840s, but the biggest wave was from the 1890s. These came mainly from Guangdong, (formerly Canton) South China, and particularly from the town of Mei Xian (Moi Yen). Some Chinese also came from Singapore and Penang. They opened provisions shops all over the island to supply the Indian labourers and, as business grew, they sent for relations in China to man their expanding enterprises. Many of the last batch of immigrants, who arrived in the first quarter of this century, are still alive. A great number of the Chinese who later ended up in Réunion, the Seychelles, Madagascar and South Africa had gone first to Mauritius.

The earlier immigrants were mostly Cantonese, the later ones Hakka. On arrival in Mauritius, the first language they had to learn - very quickly so as to be able to work in the shops - was Creole. As shopkeepers in villages where most of their customers spoke Bhojpuri, most soon also learnt to speak that language fluently.

It was common practice for Chinese men to seek work abroad and leave their wives behind until they had saved enough money to send for them. Single men would return to China to marry, but in Mauritius some married local women, generally Creoles, and their children started life speaking Creole.

Today they are known as **Creole-Sinoi**, and because very few spoke Chinese the pure Chinese called them 'half-brain'. Many old-fashioned Chinese, including some who had married Creoles, believed that their children should be brought up the Chinese way and sent their offspring to China for their education and to learn about its culture.

While most first-generation parents spoke Chinese to their children and sent them to local Chinese schools, the practice seems not to have survived beyond the second generation. By the 1950s parents might speak to their children in Chinese, but not all the children replied in that language. Already they were finding Creole easier, even at home, however much it was frowned upon by their elders.

Today, in households where both parents are of Chinese descent, their children may understand Hakka but usually cannot speak it, particularly where the parents are Mauritian-born. As for Mandarin, only the few who studied it at school can read and speak it. There are very few Cantonese speakers in the whole Chinese population of some 25,000.

Chinese words did not really enter the Creole language until 'not-too-Chinese' restaurants, to which the locals might be attracted, opened. Egg noodles was one of the first dishes to appeal to the islanders and soon they were ordering it by its Chinese name - **chow minn**. That was in the 1950s. Other dishes were then discovered, and their names Creolized.

Some Chinese, particularly the women who did not go out to work and socialized only with other Chinese, still cannot pronounce their children's Christian names properly. For example, Jacques is **Yac** and Isabelle is **Iyabé**. In Creole, "My son Richard has become a doctor" is **Mo garson Risard finn vinn ene doctaire**, but Richard's old mother, after over 50 years in Mauritius, may still say: **Mo gasson Icha li loctaire**.

OTHER LANGUAGES

The Dutch, French and lastly the English imported slaves from several countries, and the many from the continent of Africa spoke different languages. Bantu, which is given as the origin of certain Creole words, is not a single African language but the name of a large group of languages spoken by the peoples of South and Central Africa. Slaves from Senegal spoke Wolof, from Mozambique, Swahili and from Madagascar, Malagasy. Communication must have been very difficult until they learned Creole, with orders from their masters being given mainly in sign language.

Although Senegal was France's first colony in West Africa, they brought fewer slaves from that country than from Mozambique or Madagascar. No trace of Wolof is evident in Creole. It is intriguing to note that today some fully negroid people are still called **Creole mazanbic** when no other slaves from Africa are known just by the name of their country. Perhaps all they could say when they first arrived in Mauritius was "Mozambique", meaning that was where they were from and the other slaves referred to them as "those from Mozambique". Several Malagasy words have become Creolised, the best known being a word most Mauritians must utter at least once a day - **mazavarou** - chilli sauce.

Since Independence, successive governments of Mauritius have invited foreigners to invest in Mauritius and today there are factories and other businesses owned and run by people of various nationalities from Europe and the Far East. They alone must have doubled the number of languages currently spoken on the island and it cannot be long before some words from their languages enter Creole. This can only enrich the living language. Mauritians may be prone to following the French in many things but one thing they are not likely to do is discourage the infiltration of foreign words into Creole, as the French government has tried to do so unsuccessfully in France.

THE CONTINUING ASCENDANCY OF FRENCH

We live in an age when there has been an enormous expansion in the learning of the English language throughout the world. Even in former French or Portuguese colonies in Africa, there has been a complete rethinking of their foreign language learning to give more importance to English. In France itself English is the most widely known foreign language and more people are learning it. Paradoxically, in Mauritius, a former British colony, the country is going in the opposite direction. Since Independence in 1968, French has steadily gained supremacy over English.

French is no longer the language of the elite and even some shop-keepers insist on speaking to you in French - provided you look sufficiently well-dressed! Naturally the islanders speak French with a Mauritian accent, with the syllables over-stressed and a wider range of pitch than the French. It also sounds quite different to the French spoken in the sister island, Réunion or to the one spoken in further afield Seychelles. But good, written 'Mauritian' French can perhaps only be detected through the use of some old French words no longer used in modern France.

To some extent all this should not be surprising in a country where French has been spoken without interruption since 1815. It is its linguistic heritage, as Creole is intrinsically linked with French. The similarity of the two languages also makes it easier for school children to learn French than English. Perhaps too, the islanders cling to the romantic if out-dated idea of French as the erstwhile language of diplomacy and European aristocracy. According to Mauritian writer Gilbert Ahnee, "Speaking French is a Mauritian's inalienable right, it is part of our soul".

No Mauritian has written about the English language with such passion! To the average islander, English is the language of the law-makers and the educationalists; it is a foreign language. 30 years after Independence, French still predominates on the island. Visitors to Mauritius today could be forgiven for sometimes thinking they were in a French colony. Newspapers, shop signs, street names and so on are mostly in French. Press advertisements, especially in the classified sections, are almost 100% in French.

According to Shiv K. Trishul, "Many people in France are making desperate efforts to delay the demise of French as a world language." Is this why, in the Indian Ocean, France is giving Mauritius more attention than, say, Madagascar or the Comoros, where the threat of English is less?

It is a fact that throughout the 158-year rule of the British, France maintained close ties with Mauritius and since Independence has continued to be generous with financial aid and cultural and educational support.

The number of presidential visits Mauritius receives from French Presidents is proof that France is still keen to encourage a close relationship with Mauritius and to increase French influence further. François Mitterrand was a frequent visitor and during one such visit in 1990 he said: "*Je voudrais établir un type de relations plus proches, plus réelles, plus vivantes ... Je suis frappé par la proximité de nos mentalités, proximité culturelle entre Maurice et la France ... si loin les uns des autres par la géography et pourtant si proches par la culture.*"

If the French feel that the status of their language is threatened in Mauritius or that there is a race for linguistic supremacy, Mauritians should not go out of their way to change that view! After all, how many people can recall the last time when a British Prime Minister in office visited Mauritius?

Mauritians are rightly appreciative of the efforts France has made to keep French influence alive in Mauritius and the present situation could be seen as just reward for them. The French have spent millions to try to keep Mauritius French. The work of the *Alliance Française* in Mauritius - incidentally the oldest branch of this institution in the world outside France - has been vitally important in maintaining high standards of French teaching on the island. So has the large number of university scholarships provided by the French government. At one time the majority of Mauritian students came to the UK for their further education, but increased fees finally made it prohibitive for them. Now most of them go to France, where university education is available to them free. Thus generations of graduates have been returning home to Mauritius who are more French in their outlook, drive French cars, drink French wine, communicate in French and want their children to have a French education.

It was partly in response to this trend that the Lycée Labourdonnais was opened. This school follows the French system of education and teaches English as a foreign language. It became one of the most sought after private schools for the children of professional people and could not satisfy demand. There are now three such schools.

Even under British rule, the non-French population of mixed races was becoming 'more French than the French'. It was from that group that the intellectuals of the country emerged, from top civil servants to judges, lawyers, doctors and teachers.

The French population declined this century, with many emigrating to South Africa and the then Rhodesia. In the years leading to and soon after Independence, thousands more went to Australia or returned to France. It can be said that in the 20th century it was perhaps these 'educated' Creoles who kept the French language going as the number of French people dwindled. They assimilated everything French: their culture, mores, life style and in particular their language. They would speak only French among themselves and at home. They would not be heard speaking Creole in public, a language they looked down on.

Hence to this day our best writers write in French and are mostly Creoles. Some who achieved success as French writers and poets in Mauritius as well as in France and other Francophone countries include Robert-Edouard Hart, Léoville l'Homme, Savinien Mérédae, Auguste Esnouf, Marcel Cabon, Marcelle Lagesse, Jean-Georges Prosper, Malcolm de Chazal, Marie-Thérèse Humbert, Edouard Maunick and the brothers Loys and André Masson. Many in this list are winners of international literary prizes. As they could have reached a far greater readership if they had written in English, the fact that they had not done so must be because they express themselves better in French.

At one time it was true to say that Creoles were better at writing in French while the Indians preferred English as their medium of expression. Or as Vicram Ramharai put it: "The coloured people chose French language to defend their rights and their cultural heritage, the Indians used English ... to make themselves heard by the authorities at the beginning of the 20th century." This is no longer the case. Which language a writer chooses to write in is not decided by their ethnic origin. Two Indo-Mauritians who have achieved recognition writing in French are Hassam Wachill and Vinesh Hookooms-ingh. There are now also some talented Mauritians who are equally at home in either language, such as Régis Fanchette and Joseph Tsang Mang Kin.

THE FUTURE OF ENGLISH IN MAURITIUS

The trouble with the English language in Mauritius is that, unlike French, there is really no distinct group fighting its corner. The British Council does its best but it was threatened with closure a couple of years ago and its budget will probably decrease rather than increase. The British, after all, have more ex-colonies than the French to support. In any case, had they tried to influence linguistic policy after granting independence to Mauritius, it could have been interpreted as interference - something the French are less likely to be accused of in Mauritius. So the supremacy of French goes unchallenged on the island.

If Mauritius is serious about being a continuing economic success and a country to be reckoned with, it cannot afford to neglect the English language just because everybody speaks French. Nor should the Mauritians expect England to be as generous as France in supporting the language. Mauritians themselves should recognise the enormous value of English to their country, not only for its economic future, but also culturally, intellectually and in its relationship with the outside world. English is the language of commerce and diplomacy, the medium of international communication. In Mauritius it also has the added advantage of not being associated with any class or ethnic group. Whilst it may never be as popular as French, unlike the latter it is a neutral language which is acceptable to all. A former director of the

111

British Council in Mauritius, Michael Bootle, once said: "English has the advantage and disadvantage in Mauritius of being the language of everyone and of no-one."

With so many languages spoken on the island, the islanders must have a particular gift for learning languages. But being the pragmatic people that they are, in addition to some inherent laziness, they seem to bother to learn a language only when they can see a direct benefit. For example, hotel staff and people involved in tourism and commerce have no problem learning English. But the standard is not what it could be. It should be a lot better and it is defeatist of them to say that they can get by with what they know.

Perhaps it is this attitude of the adults towards the English language that is responsible for Mauritian school children dreading English as a subject. This fear is reflected in their disappointing exam results year after year. Lack of motivation is a problem but perhaps a bigger obstacle is the teaching method, often in French! Many English classes are taught by teachers who are themselves hardly fluent in English and who have never been taught the language properly. Very often these teachers have only just passed their A level in English literature when they find themselves teaching Shakespeare! Also it is time that students stop using the excuse that it is easier to learn French than English as the former is closer to Creole.

Despite what official literature keeps repeating when giving information about Mauritius, English is apparently not the official language of the country. Its Constitution merely states that English is the language to be used officially in the Assembly. This was confirmed by a senior judge, Robert Ahnee: *"Je ne connais aucun texte de loi qui dit que l'Anglais est la langue officielle de l'île Maurice"*. Note that this is deliberately said in French. (I know of no aw which states that English is the official language of Mauritius). According to some Mauritian Francophiles, French is *"la langue officieusement officielle"*. Whether or not English has any official status or is considered unofficially as the official language of the country, it is the language of official communication and civil servants are officially supposed to communicate in it.

To return to the subject of whether English has a future in Mauritius, the conclusion must be yes. But it may be another generation before the average Mauritian speaks English with the same confidence as he does French. The people responsible for this being so could well be school children, that increasing group of Mauritian children who find speaking in English comes naturally to them.

These are the children of Mauritians who were born in English-speaking countries while their parents were living there and have now returned home. Their mother tongue or first language is English. It is not unusual to find Mauritian parents in countries such as England who prefer that their children speak English at home as they regard Creole as a "useless language which will not serve any purpose outside Mauritius". Back in Mauritius they want their children to retain that English and speak to them in that language. Other school children, seeing the ease with which they speak the 'dreaded' language, may begin to lose their fear and make an extra effort to emulate their 'foreign' fellow pupils.

There are also other things which are now taking place in Mauritius which augur well for the expansion of English there. One is the opening of 'international' schools, such as Le Bocage, a school which teaches in English and follows the British private school system. Then there are Mauritians who are settled in English-speaking countries such as Australia, Canada and the UK who go to Mauritius for holidays.

Their children speak English, which their Mauritian cousins and friends envy; they also have to make the effort to speak to the visitors in English. All this goes to make English more popular. It is these Mauritians who have lived abroad who are partly responsible for so many English words entering Creole in the last decade or so. They tend to use English words where there are no Creole equivalent, such as: **To pa mind?** - You don't mind? Other words they have introduced to Creole are baby-sitter, job, sale, suntan, bye bye, daddy, sorry, all these have been Creolised. Information technology and pop songs are also responsible for the increase of English words in Mauritian Creole, as is the case with some other languages. Clearly Mauritians do not object to using the odd words in English, what they do not like is having to learn to speak and write it properly.

Finally, it is most encouraging to see the media using more English. Until a few years ago, there was hardly any English in the local papers, apart from legal notices and official communiques, and what little English was published was poor and probably did more harm than good. Now some reprint specialist features taken from English newspapers and magazines as well as commission articles by English journalists, especially in the business sections. Even certain advertisements in the papers now appear in English. For example, for professional or jobs demanding better qualifications or in IT, where good English is a necessary requirement. Also those advertising electronic and computer equipment. There are now more opportunities to read English with the increased availibility of English newspapers on the island. Unfortunately Mauritian English-only publications must still find it hard to gain sufficient readership as a few have been launched but been shortlived. One exception is perhaps the weekly *Mauritius Times,* now in its fourth decade. It has probably survived because it has published more and more items in French.

Mauritian writers are also gaining more confidence and an increasing number now write in English. In 1997 a British publisher, Flambarb Press, published a collection of short stories in English by Mauritian writers living in Mauritius, entitled *Mauritian Voices*. Professional Mauritian authors who have achieved success writing in English are still rare. They include Jay Narain Roy, Kissoonsingh Hazareesingh and Azize Asgarally.

WHITHER CREOLE?

Creole is now the undisputed lingua franca of Mauritius. One reason why it has survived all the odds to achieve this position is due to its simplicity, its flexibility and the fact that it has no syntactic rules, no verbs, no grammar and, as it was not a written language, has no spelling to learn. Today's visitors to the island find the language easy to pick up and they have no inhibition in speaking it knowing that they cannot make grammatical mistakes.

Before looking at where Creole is going, let us look back to its beginning and look at how one Bantu word, **sega,** may have played an important role in the success of Creole as a language. The book *Sega: The Mauritian Folk Dance* describes how this word has evolved.

"Freycinet noted that '*chéga ou plutot tchéga'* was the name of a dance from East Africa as well as a general word for tunes composed by slaves. Arago wrote that the *tchéga* of Mauritius was like the dance called *chica* he had seen performed by slaves in Brazil a few months earlier. The *chica* is also danced in Haiti and Martinique.

"The spelling adopted by these Frenchmen may seem strange but they were also used by Mauritian writers of the time alongside *tiéga* (Chrestien, 1822), *tschiéga* (D'Unienville, 1838), *céga* (Descroizilles, 1867) and the familiar *séga* (Baissac, 1880).

"The origin of sega is a widespread Bantu verbal root meaning 'play' and, by extension, 'dance', 'have a good time', 'laugh'. It is interesting to note that the Creole word has the sense of 'play' in the phrase '**Pa faire to sega are moi'** - 'Don't play around with me' ".

The practice of dancing and singing sega started in Mauritius when, at the end of a day's hard work, some slaves would gather round a fire on the beach to relax and talk about their day. Some drinking of their home-made **arrak** probably took place and the little gathering would more likely than not end with some singing and dancing as was their tradition back home. Their means of communication was a sort of broken French, picked up from listening to their French masters. It was the incorporating of this French patois into their sega songs which turned sega into the 'rallying cry' of the slaves.

Sega became the medium through which news travelled across the island. The lyrics were about their plight, the cruelty of their masters, their longing for home, perhaps about the devastation of the last cyclone or even stories of those who managed to escape. Wherever Creole was spoken, sega went. As sega spread to the neighbouring islands: Rodrigues, Réunion, Seychelles and other dependencies of Mauritius such as Diego Garcia, Agalega and St Brandon, so did sega. Being able to understand Creole meant being able to understand and sing sega. Hence where the language was not spoken, as in Madagascar, for example, which is nearer to Mauritius than some of the other islands, there is no sega. Creole was therefore crucial to the success and survival of sega and sega in turn was, to some extent, instrumental in ensuring the popularity and continuity of Creole.

Happily, that early sorrowful music of the slaves is today a vibrant music of rejoicing and the lyrics are now about love, courting and drinking. What was once looked upon as a retrogade activity and frowned upon by the Catholic Church is today, just like the Creole language, an essential aspect of Mauritian culture that unites all the races - everybody loves sega.

As a living language, Mauritian Creole is changing and evolving all the time. No regional variations have been noticed, which is not surprising considering how small the island is. The current subtle change the language is undergoing is that some 'more French educated' Mauritians, for want of a better term, are trying to 'improve' it. These people speak Creole by pronouncing the French parts of the language 'properly', that is as if they were speaking French, although they do not attempt to speak it in a grammatically correct way such as trying to conjugate the verbs. For example, "It's hot today despite being only 4 November," in Creole is: **Zordi faire so mem qui li encor cat novem,** would become **Aujourdui faire chaud meme qui li encor quatre novembre.** In other words they pronounce their 'ch', 'j' and 'g' properly and add on the missing part of a truncated French word, as **aujourd'hui** for **zordi** and **novembre** for **novem**. This 'refined' Creole is regarded by some as pompous or a sign of affectation, unless, of course, the speaker happens to be Franco-Mauritian, for whom it may be natural to speak like that.

Then there is the practice of using a correct French word for one which is used 'incorrectly' in Creole. A few examples will make this clear. "A nice song" in Creole is **ene zoli santer**, in 'corrected' Creole it becomes **ene zoli sanson**. Similarly, "I'll meet you there", **moi zoinne toi laba**, becomes **moi rencont toi laba** and "I've received a letter", **mo finn gagne ene let** is changed into **mo finn recevoir ene let**. This practice is, however, spreading faster than the locals are realising - it is the overseas Mauritians who seem to notice these differences!

More Creole written in gallicized orthography is used in private letters than would be admitted. An anecdote would illustrate this. In the late 1970s, thanks to the generosity of the then USSR government, many Mauritians students were offered scholarships to study in the Soviet Union. The offer of free tertiary education had a 'price' - loss of privacy. Not only were newspapers and other literature sent to the scholars by their friends and families intercepted and certain articles censored, so were private letters. The latter, however, posed a problem to the scrutineers. Whereas the publications were either in English or French, many of the letters contained passages in Creole. The Russians just could not decipher the frequent appearance of this strange language. So the students would be given back their letters with the parts in Creole heavily obliterated with a thick black felt pen.

Could the popularity of Creole bring its downfall? Are some speakers of Bhojpuri jealous of the universal acceptance of Creole in Mauritius - at the expense of their ancestral language? There is no longer any stigma attached to speaking Creole and those who do are no longer regarded as 'uneducated'. Even the Franco-Mauritians are quite happy to speak it.

There are certain movements in Mauritius which want to 'glorify' Creole even further. These are groups of people who believe that Creole should be given greater importance and should be formalised into a written language. Among these are the **Komite Kordinasyon Anti Imperialis** and the **Ledikasyon pu travayer**, who are campaigning for Creole - or Kreol, as they prefer to spell it - to be adopted as the official language of the country.

The pro-Creole groups argue that Creole is the first language of most islanders, one in which they are completely at home and as such it should receive official recognition. They want to see all legislation, legal documents, contracts, official reports, notices and so on translated into Creole as of right. One of their successes may be the declaration by some members of the judiciary that they would like to see some court proceedings conducted in Creole in the interest of justice. If Creole is the only language an accused, or indeed any victim or witness, speaks and understands, then legal arguments in English must sound like double Dutch to them. In fairness to the legal system, translaters have always been provided where necessary.

The pro-Creole lobby say that French is not a Mauritian language and English will never be one. They believe that using Creole as a teaching language will help the least able, who are unfairly handicapped by having to learn two foreign languages at the outset when they already have a mother tongue, Creole.

The majority of Mauritians are against formalizing Creole into a written language with rules and see it as a retrogade step. They have no sympathy for the minority who want to turn a language which is 75% French into something as different to it as possibe, such as replacing the letter 'c' into 'k', 'i' into 'y' and 'h' into 'e'. It would be so much simpler just to study French, for which all the teaching materials they need are already available. Formalizing Creole would require a systemic way of writing, spelling and pronounciation to be agreed on and teaching materials developed. And as the vocabulary of Creole is limited, a great deal of new words would have to be 'borrowed' from other languages or invented to cover those vast areas of knowledge and learning that do not exist in Creole. The saddest part of all this is it will not make Creole more Mauritian.

Those against the idea see another danger. After having spent the most vital years of their education becoming literate in a 'manufactured' language, school children will have to switch to English and French in order to continue their schooling. So they will start learning these two important languages much later in their school life, which can only handicap them unnecessarily. Even if they get a certificate to show they are proficient in the new Creole, how will that benefit them? They will still be restricted to using it among Creole-speaking people in the region only - which they can already do perfectly well without having to spend years learning the unnecessary business of writing it. One thing they will still not be able to do is communicate in writing with people in other Creolophone countries as they have no written, formalized Creole or one that is compatible with Mauritian Creole.

The examples of written Creole produced by the pro-Creole groups seen so far do not look very promising at all - it is no exaggeration to say that it is 'torture' to read it. Proof of this is available in the number of publications which have come out in Creole and promply closed down. The weekly **L'Eppé** was probably the first modern, entirely Creole, publication to see the light in the 1950s. It did not last very long. Since then others have come and gone. The reason must be Mauritians like their Creole spoken and not read. There is an abundance of good publications in French, which is far easier to read for most Mauritians. It remains to be seen how long the latest, **La voix kreol**, published by **Muvman Morisyen Kreol Afrikin**, will last.

In their endeavours to formalize Mauritian Creole, the group **Ledikasyon pu travayer**, which is one of the most active in the pro-Creole campaign, has published poems, plays and novels in Creole. It has also translated Shakespeare and La Fontaine, among others, into the language. Even the Bible has been translated. The anti-Creolites cannot see what can be achieved in translating famous literary works into a manufactured language. They ask who in their right mind, if they can read French, would want to struggle to read the Bible in Kreol. It is difficult enough to understand as it is!

This is a debate that has no end and every effort should be made to ensure it is contained. People can get very passionate where languages are concerned, especially where too much emphasis is placed on ethnicity, as could be the case in Mauritius. We have seen what has happened in other countries where a language issue has got out of control. Its result is always divisive. Mauritius has already experienced a heated, months-long debate about the teaching of Oriental languages in primary schools, which in the end was partly responsible for a general election being called in 1995.

So long as Creole is accepted by all as a common language which is not identified with any ethnic group; is not given special status such as making it the official language of the country; is not regarded as superior to other ethnic languages and no-one is forced to learn it - then all should be well. That is exactly the status quo. But if each community starts to demand that their particular language should be recognised officially, such as Bhojpuri, on the ground that it is the language of the majority of Indians, and should be the dominant language, then the country will be treading on dangerous ground. One can see, for a start, each group demanding more radio and TV air time, and before too long the broadcasting media could become a linguistic battlefield. How a language issue can flare up may be illustrated by a recent event. The Bank of Mauritius issued new bank notes in November 1998 and it was noticed that the Tamil script of the denomination, which has always been in second place, after that in English, had been moved. Hindi had been put in its place. The Tamil community regarded this a "relegation from second to third place". To them that position was as unchangeable "as a colour upon a national flag has a particular fixed place." In the end the government was forced to withdraw the new notes to prevent serious ethnic disturbances.The safest policy is, if it ain't broke, don't mend it. The people of Mauritius should heed the wise counsel of their first Prime Minister, Sir Seewoosagur Ramgoolam: "In a fragile society like Mauritius, one should not play around with language, culture and religion."

Currently Mauritius basks in happy multilingualism with Creole as the language of everyone and those who are fortunate enough to have another language are given every encouragement to keep it alive. This does not make them any more or less Mauritian - in fact whatever or however many languages they speak, they are first and foremost Mauritian. Creole has come to be accepted as a useful and unifying language that has evolved naturally over the years without any official interference or encouragement.

How popular and acceptable it has become can be gauged by the fact that it is even used regularly at Catholic Masses. Not so many years ago, only French was good enough for priests to preach in the house of God. But even with the help of the Almighty, there was doubt that every one in the congregation understood every thing the priest said in French. Most of the people attending Masses in small villages were not French-speaking Mauritians but the poor and the uneducated. Creole has now become a language that all Mauritians can be proud of.

It is not just in the Church that people have discovered the value and advantage of Creole as a language. When Creole was first tried out in radio advertisements, everyone involved was pleasantly surprised to find an improved response. A dialogue in Creole to sell something proved superior at getting the message across. It was simply more natural than French and not a 'cheaper' language that would 'devalue' the goods being advertised. It certainly was more colourful. After all it is the language of the people *and* that of trade. Playwright Dev Virahsawmy has also proved with his plays in Creole, that the language makes a splendid vehicle for the Mauritian oral tradition.

With Creole, French and English the Mauritians now have three useful, classless languages that are acceptable to all. The best course is to leave things be, with English as the commercial, administrative and educational language. French as the social as well as an educational tongue while Creole is the preferred everyday *spoken* language of everyone.

MAURITIAN INTERNATIONAL

This is a specialist Mauritian periodical which has been published in London since 1964. Originally entitled **Voice of Mauritians**, the magazine now has a worldwide readership.

It is published quarterly in January, April, July and October and is written mostly in English, with some French and Creole. Edited by **Jacques K. Lee**, **Mauritian International** has built up a reputation for its impartial coverage of general news and features about Mauritius and Mauritians and has been described as "the keeper of Mauritius' conscience from afar".

The magazine covers Mauritian current affairs, political events, economy, history, culture, personalities, news of expatriates and reviews of new books on Mauritius. Its regular **Philatelic Corner**, now in its third decade, is written by Peter Ibbotson, *the* authority on Mauritian philately.

Subscription for three years (12 issues) to **Mauritian International** is: UK £12, Europe £18, worldwide £22. Copies are sent overseas by air mail. Cheque payable to **Nautilus Publishing Co** must be in sterling drawn on a London bank.

Mauritian International
P O Box 4100 London SW20 OXN England
Tel 0181 947 1912   Fax 0181 947 1912
Email: npc@mauritiusukworld.co.uk

DICTIONARY

ENGLISH-CREOLE

A

A a/an	ene
abcess	absé
able, to be	capave
about	apépré, environ
above	lor, laho
abroad	lotpéy
absolutely	absolimen
abuse, to	abizer
accelerator	accélérataire
accent	accen/laccen
accept, to	accepter
accident	acciden
accommodation	lozemen
accompany, to	accompagne
accountant	contab
ache, to	faire mal
acquaintance	connaissance
acre	arpen
across	lot coté
actor	actaire
address	ladresse
adult	adilt
adventure	laventire
advertisement	réclame, lannonce
advice	conseil
afraid	gagne perre
after	apré
afternoon, in the	dan lapré midi
again	encor ene cou
against	conte
age	laze
agency	lazence
agent	azen
air	lair
air mail	par avion
airplane	avion
airport	laréopor
alcohol	lalcol
alive	vivan
all	tou
allergy	alairzi
allow, to	permette
almost	presqué
alone	selle
already	dèza
also	aussi
altogether	tou ensemb
always	tou létan
ambulance	lambilance
among	parmi
amount	montan
amusement	lamizemen
and	et, ek
anger	laraze, colaire
angry	arazé, en colaire
animal	zanimo
annoy, to	annouy
another	ene lot
answer	réponse
antiseptic	antiseptic
antique	antic/antiquité
any	ninporte
anybody/anyone	ninporte qui
apartment	flat, lapartmen
appendix	lapendicit
appetite	lapéti
apple	pom
appointment	rendévou
April	avril
architect	arcitec
area	granderre, rézion
arm	lébra
arrive, to	arrive/arriver
ask, to	dimane
aspirin	aspirinne
asthma	las
at	cote
attractive	zoli
aubergine	brinzelle
aunt	tantine, matante
Australia	Lostrali
autumn	lotone
average	moiyin
avocado	zavoca
avoid, to	evit
away	pa la

B

baby	tibaba	**big**	gran, gro
back	lédo	**bill**	bil, ladition
bad	mauvai, pa bon	**bird**	zoizo/zozo
bad luck	mofinne	**birth**	naissance
bag	sac	**birthday**	laniversaire
baggage	bagaze	**biscuit**	biscui
bakery	boulanzer	**bite, to**	mord/morder
balcony	balcon	**bitter**	amer
ballpen	biro	**black**	noir
banana	banane	**bladder**	vési
bandage	bandaze	**blanket**	molton
bank	labanque	**bleed, to**	sainnier
bar	bar	**blind**	aveg
barber	coiffaire	**blister**	clos
basket	panier, tente	**blood**	disan
bat	*(animal)* sauvesouri	**blouse**	blouze
	(sport) raquette	**blue**	blé
bathe, to	bainier	**boat**	bato
bathroom	lasaldébain	**body**	lécor
bath tub	bainoir	**boil, to**	boui
battery	pil; *(motor)* batri	**bone**	lézo
beach	laplaze	**bonnet** *(car)*	capote
bean	zarico	**book**	liv
beard	labarb	**bookshop**	librairi
beautiful	zoli	**boot** *(car)*	box
because	parcequi	**bottle/half bottle**	bouteil/sopine
bed	lili	**bougainvillea**	bougainvil
bedroom	lasam dormi	**box**	boite
bee	mous dimiel	**boy**	garson
beef	bef	**bracelet**	bracelet
beer	labierre	**brain**	lacervel
before	avan	**brake**	frein
beg, to	siplier	**brass**	cuive
beginning	commencemen	**bread**	dipain
behind	derrierre	**bread fruit**	fri a pain
Belgium	Belzique	**break, to**	casser
believe, to	croire	**breakfast**	tidézéner
below	enba	**breast**	tété, sein
belt	sangue	**breathe, to**	respirer
bet	parriaze, pari	**breeze**	labrize
better	plibon	**bribe**	gous
between	ent	**bridge**	pon
beware	attention	**bring, to**	amener
bicycle	bicyclette	**bronchitis**	bronsit
		brothel	loca

brother	frère
brown	maron
brush	bros
bucket	séo
building	batimen
bulb (*light*)	globe
bundle	paquet
burn, to	briler
business	bizness, zafaire
bus	bis
bus stop	bistop
busy	occupé
but	mé
butcher	boucer
butter	diberre
button	bouton
buy, to	asté
by	par, cote

Ccabbage

cabbage	lisou
café	café
cake	gato
calendar	calendrier
camera	lapareil foto
can	1.(*v*) esqui; 2. boite
canal	canal
cancer	cancerre
cap	casket
car	loto
carburetter	carbirataire
cardamon	laiti/élaiti
carpet	tapi
carrier bag	sac, tente
carry, to	saryé
cash	cas, larzen
cassava	manioc
castle	sato
casuarina (*tree*)	filao

cat	sat
catch, to	traper
cauliflower	lisou flaire
centimetre	centimette
centipede	cenpat
centre	sant
certificate	certifica
change, to	sanzer
chain	(*ornamental*)
	lasenne
chair	sèze
chamber maid	femdésam
chameleon	camaléon
chance	sance
cheap	bon marcé
cheek	lazou
cheese	fromaze
cheque	check
chest	poitrine, ches
chicken	poul
chickenpox	varicel
child	zenfan
chilli	pima/pimen
chilli sauce	mazavarou
China	Lacine
Chinese	Sinoi
chocolate	socola
choice	soi
choke (*car*)	startaire
church	léglize
cider	cid
cigarette	cigaret
cinema	cinéma
city	lavil, envil
civil servant	fonctionnaire
clean	prop
clever	malin
client	clien
clock	réveil
closed	fermé
clothes	linze
cloud	niaze
club	clib
clutch	débréyaz
coach	bis

coat	palto désou	crow	corbo
cockerell	coq	crowd	lafoul
cockroach	cancréla	cry, to	plorer
coconut	coco	cup	tas
coffee	café	cupboard	placar
coin	piece	currency	dévize
cold	frai; *(common)*	curry	masala, carri
	lérim	curtain	rido
colic	colic	customs	ladouane
collision	colizion	cut, to	couper
colour	coulaire		
comb	peigne		
come, to	vini		
computer	computer		
concert	concerre		
condom	capot, balon anglé		
congestion	lemboutéyaz		
congratulation	félicitation		
consider, to	considerre		
constipation	constipation		
continue, to	continié	**D**aily	toulézour
contraceptive pill	pil contraceptive	damage	domaze
convenient	convénian	damp	himid
cook, to	cui; *(chef)* couzinier	dance, to	danser
cool	frai	dandruffe	tanpanne
copy	copi	dangerous	danzéré
coriander	cotomili	dark	1.somb; 2.foncé
cork	bousson	date	dat
corkscrew	tire bousson	daughter	tifi
corn	maille	day	zour
corner	contour	day time	lazourné
correct	corek, okay	dead	mor
cotton	coton	deaf	sourde
couch	sofa	dear	*(expensive)* cerre
cough, to	tousser	death	lamor
country	péy	deceive, to	couyonne, trompe
couple	coup	December	décem
cousin	cousin/e m/f	decide, to	décider
cow	vas	deep	fon
crab	crabe	deer	cerf
cramps	lacrampe	degree	dégré
crash, to	crase/craser	delay	tardé
crayfish	langouste	delicious	délicié
cream	lacrème	deliver, to	délivrer
credit	crédi	dentist	dentis

departure	dépar	draw, to	déssine
depth	profonderre	dream, to	réver
deposit	dépozit	dress	robe
desk	bireau	drink, to	boir
destination	destination	drinks	laboisson
details	détail	drive, to	condire/condirer
develop, to	(photos) dévlop	driver	soferre
dholl	dhal	driving licence	permi, licence
diabetes	diabète	drop, to	pose, flanke
diameter	diamette	drown, to	noyer
diamond	diaman	drug	drog
diarrhoea	diaré	drunk	sou
dictionary	dictionnaire	drunkard	soular
diesel	diézel	dry, to	mette sec
diet	rézime, ladiette	duck	canar
different	diféren	during	pendan
difficult	dificil	duty	dévoir
dining room	lasal a manzer	duty-free	hortax, duty free
dinner	diner		
direct, to	montrer		
directory	(tel) lannière		
dirty	sal, malang		
disabled	handicapé		
disappointed	déci		
discount	rédiction		
disease	maladi		
dish	pla		
dissatisfied	pa satisfé		
distance	distance	**E**each	sac, sacaine
dive, to	plonzer		
divide, to	divize	ear	zoreil
divorced	divorcé	earache	zoreil faire mal
dizziness	vertize	early	bonnair
do, to	faire	earrings	zano
doctor	doctaire, medcin	earwax	caca zoreil
dog	licien	east	lest
doll	poupette	Easter	Pac
donkey	bouric	easy	facil
door	laporte	eat, to	manzer
doormat	payason	ebony	ébeine/lébeine
double	doub	economical	économic
down	enba	eczema	leczéma
downstairs	enba	edge	bordire
dozen	douzaine	education	édication
draught	courandair	eel	anguy

egg	dizef	example	lexamp
eggshell	lacoq dizef	example, for	par examp
eight	huite	except	excepté
eighth	huitième	exchange, to	sanze
elastic	lastic	excuse me	exquiz moi, esquizé
elbow	coude	exhibition	exposition
electricity	électricité	exit	sorti
eleven	onze	expensive	cerre
elsewhere	ayerre	experience	lexpérience
email	email	explain, to	explique
embassy	lambassade	export, to	export
embrace, to	embrasse	extra	enplis
emergency	irzence	eye	lizié
employment	lemploa, lemploy-men		
empty	vide		
end	fini, lafin		
enemy	enemi		
engine	moterre		
engineer	inzénierre		
England	Langléterre		
English	Anglé		
enjoy, to	amize		
enough	assé	**F** face	figire
enter, to	entrer	faeces	caca
entrance	lentré	faint, to	perdi connaissance
entrance fee	pri lentré	faith	lafoi
envelop	lenvlop	fall, to	tomber
environment	lenvironmen	false	fos
epilepsy	épilepsi	family	fami
equal	égal	famous	famé
equivalent	léquivalen	fan	lévantail, ventilataire
error	érerre		
escalator	escalataire, lescalier roulan	far	loin
estate agent	coutier	fare	pri
even	mem	farm	laferme
evening	asoir	farther	pli loin
everybody	tou dimoune	fashion	lamode
everyday	toulézour	fast	vite
every one	sacaine,	fat	gro/gra m/f; (on meat) lagraiss
everything	tou		
everywhere	partou	father	papa, pa
exactly	exactémen	fault	faute
examination	lexamain	faulty	pa marcer

fax	fax, télécopi	fool	couyon
fear	perre	foot	lipied; *(measure)*
February	février		pied
fee	fré, paiemen	for	pou
feeding bottle	bibron	foreigner	étranzer
feel, to	senti	forest	laforet
feminin	féminin	forever	pou touzour, toul-
fence	barierre		tan
festival	fète	forget, to	blier
fever	lafiève	forgive, to	pardonne
few, a	ene dé	fork	fourcette
field	*(agri)* caro	form	form
fifth	cinquième	fortnight	quinzaine
fight, to	laguerre	fortunately	hérèsemen
filling station	filling	fountain	lafontaine
film	fim	four	cat
find, to	roder	fourteen	catorze
fine	*(penalty)* lamane;	fourth	catrième
	(excellent) bon	fragile	frazil
finger	lédoi	frangipani	franzipan
finished	fini	free	gratis
fire	difé	freight	frette
first	prémié	French	Francé
fish	poisson	French dressing	vinaigrette
fishing	lapes	frequent	souven
fishing rod	golette	fresh	frai
five	cinq	Friday	vendrédi
fix, to	fixer	fridge	frizidaire
flag	pavion	friend	camarade
flat	*(surface)* platte;	friendly	zenti
	(apart) flat	from	dé, sort
flea	pis	front, in/at the	divan/dévan
flesh	lacerre	fruit	fri
flight	vol	fruit juice	zidéfri
flipper	lapat canar	fry, to	frir
flood	inondation	frying pan	poilon, carail
floor	plancer, parquet;	full	plein
	(storey) létaze	funny	comic, amizan
flour	lafarine	furlong	ferlong
flower	flaire	furniture	meb
flu	lagrippe	further	plis
fly	*(insect)* mous	fuse	fizib
fly, to	envoler	future	fitire
follow, to	suive		
food	manzer		

G

G gale	diven for
gallery	galri
gallon	galon
gamble, to	zouer
gambler	zougaderre
game	zouer
garden	zardin
garlic	lail
gearbox	boite vites
germ	zerme
German	Alman
Germany	Lalmagne
get, to	gagne
gift	cado
gin	gin
ginger	zinzam
girl	tifi, mamzel
girlfriend	copine, tidiset
give, to	donne
glad	conten
glass	ver
glasses	*(spectacles)* linette
glass pane	vite
gloves	légan
glue	lacol
go, to	alle/aller
goat	cabri
God	bondié
gold	lor
golf	golf
good	bon
goodbye	aurévoir
goods	marcendiz
goose	lézoi
government	gouvernemen
gram	gram
grandfather	granpère/papa
grandmother	granmère/mama
grape	raisin
grapefruit	pamplémousse
grass	lerbe
green	ver
grey	gri
group	group

grow, to	pousser
guava	gouyave
guest	invité
guide	guide
guinea fowl	pintad

H

H haggle	marcender
hair	cévé
haircut,	taille cévé
hairdresser	coifferre
half	lamoitié, edmi
ham	zambon
hammer	marto
hand	lamé
handbag	caba
handbrake	frein a bra
handicraft	artizana
handkerchief	moussoir
handle	poinié, lamance
handsome	zoli, zoli garson
handwriting	lécritire
happy	conten
hard	dir
hare	lième
hat	sapo
hate, to	détester
have	énan
hayfever	lafième dé foin
head	latète
headache	latète faire mal
headlight	far
heal, to	guéri
health	lasanté
hear, to	tender
heart	lécaire

heat	salerre; (verb) sof	hunting	lasas
heating	sofaze	hurry, to	dégazer
heaven	léciel	hurts, it	li faire mal
heavy	lour	husband	mari, bonomme
hectare	hectar	hypertension	tension
heel	talon		
height	hoterre		
hell	lenfer		
hello	allo		
help, to	aid		
hen	poul		
her	li		
here	ici		
hers/his	pou li		
hibiscus	ibiskis		
hide, to	casiette		
high	haute	**I**ice	glasson
hill	ti montagne	ice cream	sorbet
him	li	idea	lidé
hire, to	louer	if	si
history	zistoire	ignition key	laclé contac
hobby	passtan	ill	malad
hold, to	trapper, tiombo	illness	maladi
hole	trou	image	zimaze
holiday	vacance, conzé	immediately	toud suite
honest	honette	impatient	impatien
honey	dimiel	important	importan
honeymoon	line dé mièle	in	dan, en
hoot, to	tromper	inch	pouce
hope	lespoir; (verb) es-	increase, to	augmenter
	perer	incredible	incroiyab
horrible	horib	indeed	vraimen
horse	séval/souval	Indian	Indien
horse racing	lécous séval	Indian Ocean	Océan Indien
hospital	lopital	indicator	lindicataire
hot	so	indigestion	indizestion
hotel	lotel	infant	tibaba, zenfan
hour	laire/aire	infection	infection
house/home	lacaze	infectious	contazié
how	qui manierre, co-	inflate, to	gonfler
	man	inform, to	informe
hubcap	sopinet	inhabitant	habitan
humid	himid	inhaler	linhalataire
hundred	cen	injection	pikire
hungry	gagne faim	injured	blessé

128

inquire	dimander, rrsénié	journalist	zournalis
insane	fou/folle m/f	joy	lazoi
insect	mous	juice	zi
inside	endan	July	ziliette
insomnia	pa capave dormi	jump, to	saute/r
instead	aulié	jumper	trico, poulovaire
insurance	lashirance	June	zuin
interest	lintéré	just	zis
interesting	intéréssan		
intestine	lintestin		
into	dan		
invite, to	invite		
invoice	factire		
Irish	Irlandai/se m/f		
iron	fer, caro		
iron, to	dresse		
island	lil		
it	sa, li		
Italian	Italien/ne m/f	**K**keep, to	garde/r
itch, to	gratte/gratter	kettle	boulloire
item	lartic	key	laclé
		kidney	lérin
		kill, to	touyé
		kilogram	kilo
		kilometre	kilomette
		kind	zenti
		king	léroi
Jjack	vérin	kiss, to	embrasse, ba
jacket	palto	kitchen	lacouzine
jackfruit	zac	kite	cervolan
jail	prison	knee	zénou
jam	confitire, lazlé	knife	couto
January	zanvier	know, to	connait
jaw	lamasoire	knowledge	connaissance
jealousy	zalouzi		
Jew	Zuif		
jewellery	bizou		
job	travail, job		
jogging	jogging		
joke	plaisantri, jok		

L

lace	(*shoe*) lacé; (*textile*) dentel
lake	lac
lamb	mouton
lampshade	abazour/labazour
land	laterre
land, to	attérir
landlord	propriétaire
language	langaze
large	gro, gran
last	dernier
late	tar, en rétar
later	plitar
laugh, to	riyé
lavatory	toilet
law	laloi
lawn	lapélouse
lawyer	avoca, avoué
leaf	feil
learn, to	apranne
leather	lapo, cuir
leave, to	quitter, aller
leek	poiro
left	gos
left-handed	gossé
leg	lazam
lemon	citron, limon
lemonade	limonade
lend, to	prete
length	longuerre
lentils	lenti
less	moin
lesson	lésson
let, to	louer
letter	let
lettuce	léti
library	bibliotec
life	lavie
lift	lacencerre
light	lalimierre; (*weight*) lézé; (*colour*) clair
light bulb	globe
lighter	briquet

lightning	zéclair
like, to	conten; (*prep*) comme
lip	lalev
lipstick	dirouze
listen, to	écoute
litre	litte
litter	salté
little	piti
live, to	viv, reste
liver	léfoi
living room	salon
lizard	lézar
lobster	omar
lock, to	mette laclé; (*noun*) sérire
London	Lond
long	long
look, to/look for	guetter, roder
lorry	camion
lot, a	boucou, ene cantité
lost	perdi
lounge	salon
love, to	conten
low	ba
luck, good	bonne sance
lucky	énan sance
luggage	bagaze
lunch	dézéner, lunch
lung	poumon
lychee	letsi

M

machine	macine
mad	fou/fol m/f, fouka
magazine	magazine
maggot	mootouk
maid	femme désam; nénenne
maiden name	nom zennefi
mail	let
make, to	faire
malaria	maléria
male	mal
man	zom
manager	manager
mango	mang
manner	manierre
many	boucou, ene cantité
map	map
March	marce
margarine	margarine
marijuana	gandia
market	bazar
marriage	mariaze
mass	(religion) lamess
massage	massaze
match	zalimette; (sport) match
mattress	matla
Mauritian	Mauricien
Mauritius	Maurice
May	mai
may I?	esqui mo capave?
maybe	pétette
me	moi
meal	manzer, pla
measles	larouzol
measure	mésire
meat	laviane
medicine	medcine
medium	(steak) bienfrire
meet, to	rencontre, zoinne
member	memb
mend, to	réparer
memory	mémoire
menu	méni

message	mésaze
meter	conterre
metre	mette
midday	midi
middle	aumilié
midnight	minuit
migraine	migraine
milk	dilait
mind	lespri
mine	pou moi
minister	minis
mint	lamente
minute	minit
mirror	miroir, laglace
miscarriage	fos cous
mistake	érerre
mistress	maitresse, trente cinq
misty	brimé
Monday	lindi
moment	momen
momemtum	lélan
money	larzen, cas
mongoose	mangous
monkey	zaco
month	moi
more	plis, encor
morning	gramatin
Moslem	Mizilman
mosque	mos
mosquito	moustic
mosquito bite	pikire moustic
moss	gomo
mother	mama, ma
motorcycle	motocyclette
motor oil	diluile moterre
mountain	montagne
mouth	labous
move, to	bouzer; (house) déménazer
Mr	missié
Mrs	madame
much	boucou, ene cantité
mud	labou
mudguard	gardebou

mumps	zoréyon	newspaper	lagazette
muscle	musc	next	procin
museum	mizé	nice	zoli, bien
mushroom	cenpiyon	niece	nièce
music	lamisic	night	asoir, lanuite
musician	mizicien	nine	nef
must	bizin	no	non
mustard	lamoutarde	nobody	personne
mutton	mouton	noise	tapaz, dibri
my	mo	none	nannié
		noodle	minn
		no-one	personne
		north	lénor
		nose	néné
		nosebleed	néné sainnié
		nothing	nannié
		notice	avi
		novel	roman
		November	novam
		now	maintnan
Nnail	zong; *(tech)* coulou	nowhere	aucaine par
nail polish	verni	number	niméro
naked	touni	nurse	infirmier/e m/f
name	nom		
napkin	serviette		
narrow	séré		
nationality	nationalité		
nauseous	envi vomi		
near	pré		
nearby	pré parla		
necessary	nécéssaire		
neck	licou		
necklace	colié		
need	bizin		
needle	zégoui	**O**obey, to	obéi
neighbour	voizin	obvious	éviden
nephew	névé	occupation	loquipation
nerve	ner	ocean	océan
nervous	nervé	October	octob
net	*(fishing, tennis)* filet	octopus	ourite
Netherlands	Holand	odd	drole
never	zamais	odour	loderre
new	nef	of	dé
news	nouvel,news, information	off	*(light, machine)* teigne

offend, to	offence
offer, to	offerre
office	bireau
often	souven
oil	diluile
old	vié
ometette	omlet
on	lor
on/off	alimé/teigne
once	enefoi, ene cou
one	ene
onion	zonion
only	sellemen
open	ouver
operation	opération
opinion	lopinion
opposite	en face, lopozit
optician	opticien
or	ou
orange	zoranze
orchestra	lorcaiss
order	lord; (verb) pass commane
ordinary	ordinaire
origin	lorizine
other/s	lot/lézot
ounce	once
our	nou
outside	déhor
oven	four
over	fini
overdone	tro cui
owe, to	doi
owner	propriétaire
oyster	zuite

P

padlock	cadna
pail	séo
pain	doulaire, faire mal
paint	lapeintire
paint brush	pinso
painting	tablo, peintire
pale	pal
papaya	papaye
paper	papier
pardon	pardon, sorry
parent	paren
parking	parking
parsley	persi
partner	partnaire
party	parti
passenger	passazé
passion fruit	grénadine
passport	passpor
past	lépassé
pastry	lapate
pavement	trotoir
payment	paiemen
peace	lapai
peach	pes
peacock	pan
peanut	pistas
peas	tipoi
pebble	cayou
pedal	pédal
pedestrian	piéton
pedestrian crossing	crosseer, passaze clouté
pen	plime
penalty	lamanne
pencil	crayon papier
penknife	canif
pensioner	pensionnaire
people	dimoune
pepper	dipoive
perfume	parfin
perhaps	pétette, quit foi
person/s	dimoune
pest	(person) enmerdère
petrol	lessence

petrol station	filling	post office	lapos
pharmacy	lafarmaci	potato	pom dé terre
photo	foto	poultice	coyok
phrase	fraze	pound	(*weight/sterling*) liv
pickled	confi	power	(*authority*) pouvoir
picture	portré	prawn	camaron, cévrette
pig	cosson	pray, to	prier
pigeon	pizon	prayer	laprierre
pill	pilil	prefer	préferre
pillow	lorier	pregnant	enceinte
pillowcase	tédorier	prescription	lordonance
pilot light	véyez	present	(*gift*) cado
pineapple	zanana	press, to	(*clothes*) dress
pink	rose	pretty	zoli
pipe	lapip	prevent	evite
pity	pitié	price	pri
place	lendroi	pride	fierté
plane	avion; (*tool*) rabo	priest	prète
plant	plante	print, to	imprime
plate	lasiette, pla	private	privé
play, to	zouer	prize	pri
please	sivouplé	probably	probablémen
pleasure	plaizir	problem	problem
plenty	ene cantité, boucou	produce, to	prodire
pliers	tanaille	profession	proféssion
plug	prise, plug	profit	profi
plum	prine	prohibited	pénan droi
plumber	plombier	promise	promess
p.m.	lapré midi	proof	prève
pocket	pos	property	dibien
poetry	poézi	prostitute	pitain
poinsettia	poinsétia	protect, to	protèze
pointed	pointi	proud	fier
poison	poizon	public holiday	conzé piblic
police	lapolice	publish, to	piblier
policeman	policier, garde	pull, to	hisser
pomegranate	grénade	pump	lapomp
popcorn	pokpok	pumpkin	ziromon
popular	popilaire	puncture	fit
pork	porc	purchase, to	asté
position	pozition	pure	pire
possible	posib	purse	porte monnaie
post, to	poster	push, to	pousser
postcard	carte postal	put, to	mette
postman	facterre	pyjamas	pizama

Q
qualification calification
quality calité
quarter, a ene car
queen lareine
question kession
quick vite, dégazer
quiet tranquil

R
rabbit lapin
race (*sport*) lécourse;
(*people*) ras
racket (*sport*) raquette
radiator radiataire
radio radio
rain lapli
rainbow lacanciel
raincoat pardési
rape, to viole
rare (*steak*) sainnian;
(*unusual*) rar
raspberry framboise
razor razoir
razor blade lam razoir
read, to lire
ready paré
real vrai, veritab
realize, to réalizer
reason raison
receipt réci
receive, to récevoir, ganier
recently résaman
recipe récette
recommend, to récomann

record (*gramophone*) dis;
(*sport*) récor
red rouze
reduction rédiction
refreshments laboisson
refund remboursemen
refuse, to réfise
region larézion
registered (*mail*) récomandé,
enrézistré
**registration
number** niméro loto
rehearsal répétition
relation/relative fami
religion larélizion
religious rélizié
remedy rémede
remember, to maziner, rapel
rent location, loyer
rent, to louer
repair, to réparer
representative réprésentan
reservation réservation
reserve, to réserve
responsible responsab
rest, to réposer
result rézilta
return, to rétourne
reverse, to mette arrierre, quilé
reward récompense
rheumatism rématis
rhum rom
rice diri/douri
rich ris
right (*correct*) corek;
(*side*) droite
ring (*on finger*) bag;
(*bell*) sonne
ripe mire
river larivierre
road lari
robbery vol
roof toi
room lasam
rope lacorde

rot, to	pourri	scheme	plan, prozet
round	ron	scissors	cizo
round about	ronpoin	scholarship	labourse, lauréat
row, to	*(quarrel)* laguerre	school	lécol
rubber stamp	tampon,estampe	science	sience
rubbish	salté, bagatel	scientist	sientis
rumour	rimer	Scotland	Lécos
run, to	galoupe/galouper	Scottish	Ecosé
rupee	roupi	scream, to	crier
rust	larouil	screw	vis
		screw driver	tournavis
		sculptor	sculpterre
		sea	lamer
		seafood	fridémer
		search, to	roder
		season	lasaison
		seatbelt	cintire
		second	ségon, dézième
		security	sékirité
		see, to	trouv/er
Ssad	triste, faire sagrin	sega	séga
safe	*(for valuables)* co-for; *(not danger-ous)* pénan danzer	seldom	rarman
		self-employed	travail pou limem
		self-service	self-service
salad	salad	sell, to	vand
salary	salaire, lapaye	seller	vanderre, marsan
saliva	lacrass	send, to	envoye
salmon	somon	sentence	*(grammar)* fraze
salt	diselle	separately	séparémen
same	mem, limem	September	septem
sand	disab	serious	sérié
sandals	sandal	service	servis
sandwich	sanwhich	seven	set
satisfied	satisfé	severe	séver
Saturday	samdi	sex	sex
sauce	lasauce	shade	lombraze
saucer	soucoupe	shadow	lomb
sausage	socis	shake, to	sacouyer
savage	sauvaze	shallow	pafon
saw	*(tool)* larsar	shame	lahonte
say, to	dire	shampoo	sanpooin
scales	balance	share, to	partaze
scandal	scandal	sharp	fité
scare, to	faire perre	she	li
scarf	lésarp	shelf	létazer

136

shell	coqui, coquillaze	skin	lapo
shiny	briyan	skirt	zip
ship	bato	sky	léciel
shirt	sémiz/simiz	sleep, to	dormi
shock	soc	sleepy	gagne someil
shoelace	lacé soulier	slip, to	glisser
shoe-maker	cordonier	slippers	pantouf, soulier
shoe-polish	ciraze		lacaze
shoes	soulier	slow	doucemen
shop	laboutique	small	piti, tipti
shop assistant	comi	smell	loderre
shopping	faire magazin,	smile	sourire
	shopping	smoke, to	fimé
shore	rivaze	smoker	fimerre
short	courte	snacks	gajak
shorts	caleson courte	snoek	soonouk
shoulder	zépol	snow	lanèze
shout, to	crier	so	alor
shovel	lapel	soap	savon
shower	*(bath)* dous;	socks	soset
	(rain) lapli	sofa	sofa
show, to	montrer	soft	mou
shrimp	camaron, cévrette	somebody	quicaine
shut, to	ferme	someday	ene zour
shy	timid	someone	quicaine, intel
sick	malad	something	quit soze
side	coté	sometimes	parfoi
sign	signe	somewhere	quit par
signtseeing	visit, promner	son	garson
silk	lasoi	song	santer
silly	bette	soon	biento
silver	larzen	sore throat	lagorze faire mal
similar	pareil	sorry	pardon, sorry
sin	pécé	soul	nam
since	dépi	sound	son
sing, to	santer	soup	lasoup; *(clear)*
singer	santerre		bouyon
single	célibataire, selle	sour	aig
singular	sinquilier	south	lésid
sister	saire	South Africa	Sudafric
sister-in-law	bel saire	souvenir	souvénir
sit, to	assizer	soya sauce	lasauce soy
six	sis	space	lespace
size	grossaire,	Spain	Lespagne
	dimension	spare wheel	stepné

speak, to	cause	storey	létaze
special	special, extra	story	zistoire
spectacles	linette/ninette	straight	droite
speed	vites	stranger	étranzer
spend, to	dépense	straw	lapail
spice	zépice	stream	riso
spinach	épinar	street	lari
spine	colon vertébral	strength	laforce
spoil, to	gate	string	laficel
spoon	couyerre	strong	for
sport	sport	stubborn	téti
spring	(season) printan	student	étidian
spring onion	laqué zonion	study, to	étidier
spy	espion	stupid	couyon
square	caré	style	stil
squid	moorgat	subject	suzet
stable	lékiri	subsidy	subvention
stadium	stad	succeed, to	réssi
stain	tas	suffer, to	soufrir
stairs	lescalier	sugar	disic
stale	rasi	suit	(tailored garment)
stammer, to	bégaiyer		costime
stamp	timbe, estampe	summer	lété
stand, to	diboute	sun	soleil
star	zétoile	Sunday	dimance
starch	canze	sunglasses	linette soleil
star fruit	caranbol	suntan lotion	lotion/lacrème
start, to	commence		soleil
starting point	(of a race) go	suppose	siposé
statement	déclaration	sure	sire
station	lagar	surname	nom fami
statue	estati	swallow, to	aval
stay, to	reste/r	swear, to	zourer
steak	stake	sweat, to	transpirer
steal, to	coquin	sweep, to	balier
steam	vaperre	sweet	(taste) dou;
steps	péron		(candy) bonbon
stick, to	col; (length of	sweet potato	patate
	wood - noun) baton	swelling	enflé, gonflé
stocking	léba	swim, to	nazer
stomach	lestoma	swimming pool	lapicine
stone	ros	swimsuit	mayo
stop, to	arette	switch	(electric) také
store	magazin	symptom	sintom
storm	tempette	syrup	siro

T

table	latab
table cloth	tablier
tablet	comprimé
table tennis	pinpong
tail	laqué
tailor	tayerre
take, to	pren; *(photo)* tir
talcum powder	lapoud
talk, to	cause/r
tall	gran, haute
tamarind	tamarin
tap	robinet
taste	gou
taste, to	goute
tax	tax
taxi	taxi
tea	dité
teach, to	montrer, enseigne
teacher	enseignant/e m/f
	proféssaire
tear	*(eyes)* larme;
	(verb) décire
telephone	téléphone
television	télévision
tell, to	dire
temperature	températire
tempest	tempette
temporary	temporaire
ten	dis
tenant	locataire
tennis	tennis
tent	latente
terrible	terib
test	test; *(verb)* tester
thank you	merci
that	sa
the	la, lé
theatre	théatte
theft	vol
their	zot
theirs	pou zot
them	zot, sa
then	alor
there	laba, sa

thermometer	termomette
thermos flask	terremos
these	sa
they	zot
thick	épai
thickness	épaiserre
thief	volaire
thigh	lacouis
thin	mince, maig
thing	soze
think, to	pense, croire
third	troizième
thirsty	gagne soif
this	sa
those	sa banne
thousand	mil
thread	difil
three	troi
throat	lagorze
throw, to	zette
thumb	pouce
thunderstorm	loraze
Thursday	zédi
thus	alor
thyme	ditain
tick	*(insect)* carapat
ticket	tikette, biyé
tidy	en ord
tie	cravat
tight	séré
timber	diboi
time	laire
tip	pouboire
tired	fatigué
title	chit
to	ziska
toast	tos
today	azordi/zordi
toe	lédoi lipied
together	ensemb
toilet	toilet, cabinet
toilet paper	papier toilet
tomato	pom damour
tomorrow	dimin/démain
tonight	césoir

tongue	lalang	try, to	seye
tonsils	lamidal	Tuesday	mardi
too	aussi; (excessive)	tuna	ton
	tro	turkey	dinde
tool	zouti	turn, to	tourne
tooth	léden	turtle	torti
toothache	léden faire mal	twelve	douze
toothbrush	bros a den	twice	décou, défoi
toothpaste	dentifrice	twin-bed	lilizimo
toothpick	gratte léden	tyre	larou
top	laho;(expert)		
	niméro ene		
torn	déciré		
tortoise	torti		
total	total		
touch, to	tous		
tour guide	guide touris		
tourist	touris		
towards	ver		
towel	serviette	**U** ugly	vilain
town	lavil	ulcer	ulcerre
toy	zouzou	umbrella	parasol, parapli
trade	commerce	unable	pa capave
traffic	trafic	unconscious	perdi connaissance
traffic jam	bousson, lem-	under	enba
	boutéyaz	underground	soutérain
traffic lights	robo	underneath	enba
trailer	(cinema, TV)	underpants	caleson detsou
	réclame	understand, to	compren
train	train	underwater	soumarin, emba
tranquillizer	calman		dilo
transit, in	en transit	undress, to	dézabille
translate, to	tradire	uniform	liniform
transport	transpor	university	liniversité
travel, to	voyazer	unknown	inconni
travel agent	azen voyaze	unlucky	malsance, pénan
traveller	voyazerre		sance
tray	plato	until	ziska
tree	pié	unwell	pa bien
tremble, to	trembler	urgent	irzen
trip	voyaze	urinate, to	pisser
trouble	traca	urine	pisar
trousers	long caleson	us	nou
true	vrai	use, to	servi
truth	lavérité	useful	itil

V

vaccination	vaccination
valid	valab
value	valaire
vegetable	léghime
vegetarian	vézétarien
vein	laveine
velvet	vélour
vendor	marsan
venison	laviane cerf
verandah	lavarang
very	tré
victory	lavictoire
video	vidéo
village	vilaz
vinegar	vineg
virus	viris
visa	viza
visit, to	visit
visitor	visiterre
vocabulary	vocabilaire
voice	lavoi
volume	volim
volunteer	volontaire
vomit, to	vomi
vote, to	voter

W

wage	lapaye
wait, to	attane
waiter	garson
waitress	mamzel, serveze
wake, to	lever
walk, to	marcer
wall	mirail
wallet	portefeil

want, to	oulé
war	laguerre
wardrobe	larmoire
warm	so
warning	avertismen
wart	poro
wash, to	lav
wash basin	lavabo
washing bowl	kivet
wasp	mous zaune
watch	monte
watch, to	guette
water	dilo/délo
watercress	crésson
waterfall	cascad
watermelon	mélondo
wave	vag
wave, to	faire salam
way	sémin/simé
we	nou
weak	faib
wealth	fortine
wear, to	mette
weather	létan
weather forecast	météo
Wednesday	mercrédi
wedding	mariaze
week	sémaine
weekend	weeken
weight	poi
welcome	bienveni
well	bien
west	louest
wet	mouillé
what	qui
wheel	larou
when	quand
where	qui coté, ou
whether	si
which	léquel, qui
while	pendan
white	blan
who	qui
whole	entier
whom	qui

why	qui faire		
wide	larze	**Y** yard	1. yard;
width	larzerre		2. *(school etc)*
wife	femme, madame		lacour
will, I	mo pou	year	lanné
win, to	ganier	yellow	zaune
wind	diven	yes	oui
window	lafénette	yesterday	hier
windscreen	parbrize	you/your	*(formal)* ou,
wine	divin		*(familiar)* to
windy	énan diven	young	zenne
wing	lézelle	yours	*(formal)* pou ou,
winner	ganian		*(familiar)* pou toi
winter	liverre		
wipe, to	souille		
wipers	essuiglace		
wish, to	souhaite		
with	avec, ek		
without	san		
withdraw money	tir larzen		
witness	témoin		
woman	femme, madame		
wonderful	mervéyé		
wood	diboi; *(forest)* boi	**Z** zero	zéro
wool	lalaine	zip	fermétire éclaire
word	mo	zoo	zou
work	travail		
worker	travayerre		
workshop	latélier		
world	lémorne		
worm	léver		
worry, to	tracasse/r		
worse	pire		
wound	bléshir		
wrap, to	ploye, embal		
write, to	écrire		
writer	écrivain		
writing paper	papier a let		
wrong	pa bon, pa corek		

NOTES

NOTES

NOTES

NOTES

NOTES

BIBLIOGRAPHY

ADDISON, J. & HAZAREESINGH, K., *A New History of Mauritius*, EOI, Mauritius, 1985

ALLADIN, I., *Economic Miracle in Indian Ocean*, EOI, Mauritius, 1993

ASGARALLY, I., *Littérature et révolte*, Editions le Flamboyant, Mauritius, 1985

ASGARALLY, R., *Quand montagne prend difé*, Mascarena University Publication, Mauritius, 1977

ATCHIA, M., *Sea Fishes of Mauritius*, Mauritius, 1984

BAISSAC, Charles, *Etudes sur le patois Créole mauricien*, Nancy, 1880

BAISSAC, C., *Le folklore de l'Ile Maurice*, Maisonneuve et Larose, Paris 1888

BAKER, P. & HOOKOOMSING, V., *Dictionnaire de Créole mauricien*, L'Harmattan, Paris, 1987

BAKER, Philip, *Kreol - A Description of Mauritian Creole*, Hurst, London 1972

BENOIT, Norbert, *Le Théâtre de Port Louis - de ses origines à 1922*, Vizavi, Mauritius, 1994

BENOIT, N., ed., *La vie ou les aventures de J B Tabardin dans ses voyages*, Vizavi, 1993

BHUCKORY, S., *Hindi in Mauritius*, Editions de l'Ocean Indien, Mauritius, 1988

BISSOONDOYAL, U & SERVANSING, S., ed., *Slavery in the SW Indian Ocean*, Mahatma Gandhi Institute, Mauritius, 1989

BOOLELL, Satcam, *Untold Stories*, Editions de l'Ocean Indien, Mauritius 1996

BOWMAN, L., *Mauritius: Democracy and Development in the Indian Ocean*, Westview Press, USA, 1991

BUTLIN, R., ed., *Mauritian Voices*, Flambard, UK, 1997

CARTER, Marina, *Lakshmi's Legacy*, EOI, Mauritius, 1994

CARTER, M., *Servants, Sirdars and Settlers: Indians in Mauritius*, OUP, New Delhi, 1995

CARTER, M. et al, *Colouring the Rainbow*, CRIOS, Mauritius, 1998

CHELIN, Antoine, *Une ile et son passé 1507-1947*, Mauritius, 1974

CORNIC, A., *Poissons de l'Ile Maurice*, EOI, Mauritius, 1987

DAVID, J-B. et al, *Parlez Créole*, EOI, Mauritius, 1989

DECOTTER, Nemours, *Les proverbes français expliqués avec leurs équivalents en Anglais, augmentés parfois de proverbes Créoles*, Mauritius, 1920

DE SAINT PIERRE, Bernardin, *Paul et Virginie*, Editions Garnier, Paris

DE ST PIERRE, B., *Voyage à l'Isle de France*, Edns. La Découverte, Paris, 1983

DINAN, Monique, *Une ile éclatée*, Mauritius, 1985

DINAN, M., *The Mauritian Kaleidoscope*, Mauritius, 1986

DUYKER, Edward, *Mauritian Heritage*, AMRG, Australia, 1986

DUYKER, E., *Of the Star and the Key*, AMRG, Australia, 1989

ELLIS, R., *Guide to Mauritius*, Bradt, UK, 1988

EMRITH, M., *A History of the Muslims in Mauritius*, ELP, Mauritius, 1994

FELIX, G., *Genuine Cuisine of Mauritius*, EOI, Mauritius, 1988

GERMAIN, Robert, *Grammaire Créole*, Paris, 1976

GORDON-GENTIL, A., *Le Théâtre de Port Louis - scènes*, Vizavi, Mauritius, 1994

GUEHO, J., *La végétation de l'Ile Maurice*, EOI, Mauritius, 1989
IBBOTSON, Peter, *The Postal History & Stamps of Mauritius*, RPS, UK, 1991
ITHIER, W., *La littérature de langue française à l'Ile Maurice*, Paris, 1930
JONES, P. et al, *The Best of Mauritian Cooking*, Macmillan, UK, 1986
JOURDAIN, Elodie, *Du Français aux parlers Créoles*, Klincksieck, Paris, 1958
JOURDAIN, E., *Le vocabulaire du parler Créole de la Martinique*, Klincksieck, Paris, 1956
Ledikasyon Pu Travayer, *Diksyoner Kreol-Angle*, Mauritius, 1974
LEE, Jacques, *The Nautilus and the Gang of Three*, Vintage, New York, 1983
LEE, J. K., *Sega: The Mauritian Folk Dance*, NPC, London , 1990
LENOIR, P., *Exotic Cuisine of Mauritius*, EOI, Mauritius, 1988
LY TIO FANE, Huguette, *Chinese Diaspora in the Western Indian Ocean*, MGI, Mauritius, 1985
MAHADEO, Premlall, *Mauritian Cultural Heritage*, Gold Hill Pub, Mauritius, 1995
MANNICK, Ram, *Mauritians in London*, Dodo Books, London, 1987
MAURE, André, *Souvenirs d'un vieux colon de l'Ile Maurice*, La Rochelle, 1840
MICHEL, Claude, *Notre Faune*, Mauritius, 1966
MICHEL, C., *Birds of Mauritius*, EOI, Mauritius, 1986
MOUTOU, B., *Les chrétiens de l'Ile Maurice*, Mauritius, 1996
NAGAPEN, A., *The Indian Christian Community in Mauritius*, Mauritius, 1984
NAPAL, D., *Les Indiens à l'Ile de France*, Mauritius, 1965
NAPAL, D., *British Mauritius 1810-1984*, Mauritius, 1985
NG FOONG KWONG, James., *La naissance du commerce Chinois 1826-1875*, DEA, Réunion, 1996
NG FOONG KWONG, J. & CARTER, M., *Forging the Rainbow - Labour Immigrants in British Mauritius*, CRIOS, Mauritius
NG CHEONG LUM, R., *Culture Shock - Mauritius*, Times Books, Singapore, 1997
NOEL, Karl, *L'Esclavage à l'Isle de France*, Editions Two Cities, Paris, 1991
NORTH-COOMBES, A., *La découverte des mascareignes*, Mauritius, 1979
PADYA, B., *Weather and Climate of Mauritius*, MGI, Mauritius, 1989
PITOT, Geneviève, *The Mauritian Shekel*, Vizavi, Mauritius, 1998
PROSPER, Jean-Georges, *Histoire de la littérature mauricienne de langue française*, EOI, Mauritius, 1978
RAMAN, A., *Not a Paradise - I love you Mauritius*, EOI, Mauritius, 1991
RAMDOYAL, Ramesh, *Tales of Mauritius*, Macmillan, UK, 1981
RAMDOYAL, R., *Festivals of Mauritius*, EOI, Mauritius, 1991
RAMHARAI, Vicram, *La littérature mauricienne d'expression Créole*, Editions les Mascareignes, Mauritius, 1990
ROBERTS, K. & E., *Visitor's Guide to Mauritius, Rodrigues & Reunion*, Moorlands, UK, 1992
ROY, J.N., *Mauritius in Transition*, India, 1960
RUNGOO, G., *Hindi ou Hindoustani en 24 jours*, EOI, Mauritius, 1985
SEEWOOCHURN, C, *Hindu Festivals in Mauritius*, Edn. Capucine, Mauritius, 1995
SELVON, S. et al, *Mauritius: Its People, Its Cultures*, Mauritius, 1988
VALDMAN, A., *Haitian Creole-English-French Dictionary*, Bloomington, 1981
VIRAHSAWMY, Dev, *La fimé dans lizié*, Mauritius

BOOKS ABOUT MAURITIUS

We run a mail-order-only bookshop specialising in books on Mauritius

We sell only books on Mauritius and carry the largest stock of such books outside the island

We are also the UK agent and representative for the main Mauritian publishers and leading Mauritian authors

If you wish to see a list of books currently in stock and read some of the latest reviews, visit our website

www.mauritiusworld.com

We may also be able to help you find any rare books on Mauritius which you are looking for

Nautilus Publishing Co
P O Box 4100
London SW20 OXN England
Tel 0181 947 1912   Fax 0181 947 1912
Email: npc@mauritiusukworld.co.uk